Big Data

Big Data

Understanding How Data Powers Big Business

Bill Schmarzo

WILEY

Big Data: Understanding How Data Powers Big Business

Published by
John Wiley & Sons, Inc.
10475 Crosspoint Boulevard
Indianapolis, IN 46256
www.wiley.com

Copyright © 2013 by John Wiley & Sons, Inc., Indianapolis, Indiana

Published simultaneously in Canada

ISBN: 978-1-118-73957-0
ISBN: 978-1-118-74003-3 (ebk)
ISBN: 978-1-118-74000-2 (ebk)

Manufactured in the United States of America

10 9 8 7 6 5 4 3 2 1

For general information on our other products and services please contact our Customer Care Department within the United States at (877) 762-2974, outside the United States at (317) 572-3993 or fax (317) 572-4002.

Wiley publishes in a variety of print and electronic formats and by print-on-demand. Some material included with standard print versions of this book may not be included in e-books or in print-on-demand. If this book refers to media such as a CD or DVD that is not included in the version you purchased, you may download this material at http://booksupport.wiley.com. For more information about Wiley products, visit www.wiley.com.

Library of Congress Control Number: 2013948011

About the Author

 **Bill Schmarzo** has nearly three decades of experience in data warehousing, Business Intelligence, and analytics. He was the Vice President of Analytics at Yahoo from 2007 to 2008. Prior to joining Yahoo, Bill oversaw the Analytic Applications business unit at Business Objects, Inc., including the development, marketing, and sales of their industry-defining analytic applications. Currently, Bill is the CTO of the Enterprise Information Management & Analytics Practice for EMC Global Services.

Bill is the creator of the Business Benefits Analysis methodology that links an organization's strategic business initiatives with their supporting data and analytic requirements. He has also co-authored with Ralph Kimball a series of articles on analytic applications. Bill has served on The Data Warehouse Institute's faculty as the head of the analytic applications curriculum. He has written several white papers and is a frequent speaker on the use of Big Data and advanced analytics to power an organization's key business initiatives.

His recent blogs can be found at http://infocus.emc.com/author/william_schmarzo/

You can also follow Bill on Twitter at @schmarzo.

About the Technical Editor

Denise Partlow has served in a wide variety of V.P. and Director of Product Marketing positions at both emerging and established technology companies. She has hands-on experience developing marketing strategies and "Go To Market" plans for complex product and service-based solutions across a variety of software and services companies. Denise has a B.S. in Computer Science from the University of Central Florida. She was a programmer of simulation and control systems as well as a program manager prior to transitioning into product management and marketing.

Denise is currently responsible for product marketing for EMC's big data and cloud consulting services. In that role, she collaborated with Bill Schmarzo on many of the concepts and viewpoints that have become part of *Big Data: Understanding How Data Powers Big Business.*

Credits

Acknowledgments

It's A Wonderful Life has always been one of my favorite movies. I always envisioned myself a sort of George Baily; someone who always looked for opportunities to give back. So whether it's been coaching youth sports, helping out with the school band, or even persuading my friend to build an ethanol plant in my hometown of Charles City, Iowa, I've always had this drive to give back.

When Carol Long from Wiley approached me about this book project, with the strong and supporting push from Denise Partlow of EMC, I thought of this as the perfect opportunity to give back—to take my nearly 30 years of experience in the data and analytics industry, and share my learnings from all of those years working with some of the best, most innovative people and organizations in the world.

I have been fortunate enough to have many *Forrest Gump* moments in my life—situations where I just happened to be at the right place at the right time for no other reason than luck. Some of these moments of serendipity include:

- One of the first data warehouse projects with Procter & Gamble when I was with Metaphor Computer Systems in the late 1980s.
- Head of Sales and Marketing at one of the original open source companies, Cygnus Support, and helping to craft a business model for making money with open source software.
- Creating and heading up Sequent Computer's data warehouse business in the late 1990s, creating one of the industry's first data warehouse appliances.
- VP of Analytic Applications at Business Objects in the 2000s, creating some of the industry's first analytic applications.
- Head of Advertising Analytics at Yahoo! where I had the great fortune to experience firsthand Yahoo!'s petabyte project, and use big data analytics to uncover the insights buried in all of that data to help Yahoo!'s advertisers optimize their spend across the Yahoo! ad network.
- A failed digital media startup, JovianDATA, where I experienced the power of cloud computing to bring unbelievable analytic power to bear on one of the digital media's most difficult problems—attribution analysis.
- And finally, my current stint as CTO of EMC Global Services' Enterprise Information & Analytics Management (EIM&A) service line, where my everyday job is to work with customers to identify where and how to start their big data journeys.

I hope that you see from my writing that I learned early in my career that technology is only interesting (and fun) when it is solving meaningful business problems and opportunities. The opportunity to leverage data and analytics to help clients make more money has always been the most interesting and fun part of my job.

I've always admired the teaching style of Ralph Kimball with whom I had the fortune to work with at Metaphor and again as a member of the Kimball Group. Ralph approaches his craft with very pragmatic, hands-on advice. Ralph (and his Kimball Group team of Margy Ross, Bob Becker, and Warren Thornthwaite) have willingly shared their learnings and observations with others through conferences, newsletters, webinars, and of course, their books. That's exactly what I wanted to do as well. So I've been actively blogging about my experiences the past few years, and the book seemed like a natural next step in packaging up my learnings, observations, techniques, and methodologies so that I could share with others.

There are many folks I would like to thank, but I was told that my acknowledgments section of the book couldn't be bigger than the book itself. So here we go with the short list.

- The Wiley folks—Carol Long, Christina Haviland, and especially Adaobi Obi Tulton—who reviewed my material probably more times than I did. They get the majority of the credit for delivering a readable book.
- Marc Demarest, Neil Raden and John Furrier for the great quotes. I hope the book lives up to them.
- Edd Dumbill and Alistair Croll from Strata who are always willing to give me time at their industry-leading data science conference to test my materials, and to the "Marc and Mark Show" (Marc Demarest and Mark Madsen) who also carve out time in their Strata track to allow me to blither on about the business benefits of big data.
- John Furrier and David Vellante from SiliconAngle and theCube who were the first folks to use the term "Dean of Big Data" to describe my work in the industry. They always find time for me to participate in their industry-leading, ESPN-like technology web broadcast show.
- Warren Thornthwaite who found time in his busy schedule to brainstorm and validate ideas and concepts from the book and provided countless words of encouragement about all things—book and beyond.

I'd like to thank my employer, EMC. EMC gave me the support and afforded me countless opportunities to spend time with our customers to learn about their big data challenges and opportunities. EMC was great in sharing materials including the data scientist certification course (which I discuss in Chapter 4) and the Big

Data Storymap (which I discuss in Chapter 12). EMC also gave me the time to write this book (mostly in airplanes as I flew from city to city).

I especially want to thank the customers over the past three decades with whom I have had the great fortune to work. They have taught me all that I share in this book and have been willing patients as we have tested and refined many of the techniques, tools, and methodologies outlined in this book.

I need to give special thanks to Denise Partlow, without whose support, encouragement, and demanding nature this book would never have gotten done. She devoted countless hours to reviewing every sentence in this book, sometimes multiple times, and arguing with me when my words and ideas made no sense. She truly was the voice of reason behind every idea and concept in this book. I couldn't ask for a better friend.

Of course, I want to thank my wife, Carolyn, and our kids, Alec, Max, and Amelia. You'll see several references to them throughout the book, such as Alec's (who is our professional baseball pitcher) help with baseball stats and insights. They have been very patient with me in my travels and time away from them. I know that a thank you in a book can't replace the missed nights tucking you into bed, long tossing on the baseball field or rebounding for you in the driveway, but thanks for understanding and being supportive.

Finally, I want to thank my Mom and Dad, who taught me the value of hard work and perseverance, and to never stop chasing my dreams. In particular, I want to thank my Mom, whose devotion to helping others motivated me to stick with this book even when I didn't feel like it. So in honor of my Mom, who passed away nearly 16 years ago, I will be dedicating proceeds from this book to breast cancer research, the disease that took her away from her family, friends, and her love of helping others. Mom, this book is for you.

Contents

Preface

Think Differently.

Your competitors are already taking advantage of big data, and furthermore, your traditional IT infrastructure is incapable of managing, analyzing and acting on big data.

Think Differently.

You should care about big data. The most significant impact big data can have on an organization is its ability to upgrade existing business processes and uncover new monetization opportunities. No organization can have too many insights about the key elements of their business, such as their customers, products, campaigns, and operations. Big data can uncover these insights at a lower level of granularity and in a more timely, actionable manner. Big data can power new business applications—such as personalized marketing, location-based services, predictive maintenance attribution analysis, and machine behavioral analytics. Big data holds the promise of rewiring an organization's value creation processes and creating entirely new, more compelling, and more profitable customer engagements. Big data is about business transformation, in moving your organization from retrospective, batch, business monitoring hindsights to predictive, real-time business optimization insights.

Think Differently.

Big data forces you to embrace a mentality of data abundance (versus data scarcity) and to grasp the power of analyzing all your data—both internally and externally of the organization—at the lowest levels of granularity in real-time. For example, the old business intelligence "slice and dice" analysis model, which worked well with gigabytes of data, is as outdated as the whip and buggy in an age of petabytes of data, thousands of scale-out processing nodes, and in-database analytics. Furthermore, standard relational database technology is unable to express the complex branching and iterative logic upon which big data analytics is based. You need an updated, modern infrastructure to take advantage of big data.

Think Differently.

Never has this message been more apropos than when dealing with big data. While much of the big data discussion focuses on Hadoop and other big data technology innovations, the real technology and business driver is the *big data economics*—the combination of open source data management and advanced analytics software on top of commodity-based, scale-out architectures are 20 times cheaper than today's data warehouse architectures. This magnitude of economic change forces you to rethink many of the traditional data and analytic models. Data transformations and enrichments that were impossible three years ago are now readily and cheaply available, and the ability to mine petabytes of data across hundreds of dimensions and thousands of metrics on the cloud is available to all organizations, whether large or small.

Think Differently.

What's the biggest business pitfall with big data? Doing nothing. Sitting back. Waiting for your favorite technology vendor to solve these problems for you. Letting the technology-shifting sands settle out first. Oh, you've brought Hadoop into the organization, loaded up some data, and had some folks play with it. But this is no time for science experiments. This is serious technology whose value in creating new business models based on petabytes of real-time data coupled with advanced analytics has already been validated across industries as diverse as retail, financial services, telecommunications, manufacturing, energy, transportation, and hospitality.

Think Differently.

So what's one to do? Reach across the aisle as business and IT leaders and embrace each other. Hand in hand, identify your organization's most important business processes. Then contemplate how big data—in particular, detailed transactional (dark) data, unstructured data, real-time data access, and predictive analytics—could uncover actionable insights about your customers, products, campaigns, and operations. Use big data to make better decisions more quickly and more frequently, and uncover new monetization opportunities in the process. Leverage big data to "Make me more money!" Act. Get moving. Be bold. Don't be afraid to make mistakes, and if you fail, do it fast and move on. Learn.

Think Differently.

Introduction

Big data is today's technology hot topic. Such technology hot topics come around every four to five years and become the "must have" technologies that will lead organizations to the promised land—the "silver bullet" that solves all of our technology deficiencies and woes. Organizations fight through the confusion and hyperbole that radiate from vendors and analysts alike to grasp what the technology can and cannot do. In some cases, they successfully integrate the technology into the organization's technology landscape—technologies such as relational databases, Enterprise Resource Planning (ERP), client-server architectures, Customer Relationship Management (CRM), data warehousing, e-commerce, Business Intelligence (BI), and open source software.

However, big data feels different, maybe because at its heart big data is not about technology as much as it's about business transformation—transforming the organization from a retrospective, batch, data constrained, monitor the business environment into a predictive, real-time, data hungry, optimize the business environment. Big data isn't about business parity or deploying the same technologies in order to be like everyone else. Instead, big data is about leveraging the unique and actionable insights gleaned about your customers, products, and operations to rewire your value creation processes, optimize your key business initiatives, and uncover new monetization opportunities. Big data is about making money, and that's what this book addresses—how to leverage those unique and actionable insights about your customers, products, and operations to make money.

This book approaches the big data business opportunities from a pragmatic, hands-on perspective. There aren't a lot of theories here, but instead lots of practical advice, techniques, methodologies, downloadable worksheets, and many examples I've gained over the years from working with some of the world's leading organizations. As you work your way through this book, you will do and learn the following:

- Educate your organization on a common definition of big data and leverage the Big Data Business Model Maturity Index to communicate to your organization the specific business areas where big data can deliver meaningful business value (Chapter 1).
- Review a history lesson about a previous big data event and determine what parts of it you can apply to your current and future big data opportunities (Chapter 2).

- Learn a process for leveraging your existing business processes to identify the "right" metrics against which to focus your big data initiative in order to drive business success (Chapter 3).

- Examine some recommendations and learnings for creating a highly efficient and effective organizational structure to support your big data initiative, including the integration of new roles—like the data science and user experience teams, and new Chief Data Office and Chief Analytics Officer roles—into your existing data and analysis organizations (Chapter 4).

- Review some common human decision making traps and deficiencies, contemplate the ramifications of the "death of why," and understand how to deliver actionable insights that counter these human decision-making flaws (Chapter 5).

- Learn a methodology for breaking down, or functionally "decomposing," your organization's business strategy and key business initiatives into its key business value drivers, critical success factors, and the supporting data, analysis, and technology requirements (Chapter 6).

- Dive deeply into the big data Masters of Business Administration (MBA) by applying the big data business value drivers—underleveraged transactional data, new unstructured data sources, real-time data access, and predictive analytics—against value creation models such as Michael Porter's Five Forces Analysis and Value Chain Analysis to envision where and how big data can optimize your organization's key business processes and uncover new monetization opportunities (Chapter 7).

- Understand how the customer and product insights gleaned from new sources of customer behavioral and product usage data, coupled with advanced analytics, can power a more compelling, relevant, and profitable customer experience (Chapter 8).

- Learn an envisioning methodology—the Vision Workshop—that drives collaboration between business and IT stakeholders to envision what's possible with big data, uncover examples of how big data can impact key business processes, and ensure agreement on the big data desired end-state and critical success factors (Chapter 9).

- Learn a process for pulling together all of the techniques, methodologies, tools, and worksheets around a process for identifying, architecting, and delivering big data-enabled business solutions and applications (Chapter 10).

- Review key big data technologies (Hadoop, MapReduce, Hive, etc.) and analytic developments (R, Mahout, MADlib, etc.) that are enabling new data management and advanced analytics approaches, and explore the impact these technologies could have on your existing data warehouse and business intelligence environments (Chapter 11).

■ Summarize the big data best practices, approaches, and value creation techniques into the Big Data Storymap—a single image that encapsulates the key points and approaches for delivering on the promise of big data to optimize your value creation processes and uncover new monetization opportunities (Chapter 12).

■ Conclude by reviewing a series of "calls to action" that will guide you and your organization on your big data journey—from education and awareness, to the identification of where and how to start your big data journey, and through the development and deployment of big data-enabled business solutions and applications (Chapter 13).

■ We will also provide materials for download on `www.wiley.com/go /bigdataforbusiness`, including the different envisioning worksheets, the Big Data Storymap, and a training presentation that corresponds with the materials discussed in this book.

The beauty of being in the data and analytics business is that we are only a new technology innovation away from our next big data experience. First, there was point-of-sale, call detail, and credit card data that provided an earlier big data opportunity for consumer packaged goods, retail, financial services, and telecommunications companies. Then web click data powered the online commerce and digital media industries. Now social media, mobile apps, and sensor-based data are fueling today's current big data craze in all industries—both business-to-consumer and business-to-business. And there's always more to come! Data from newer technologies, such as wearable computing, facial recognition, DNA mapping, and virtual reality, will unleash yet another round of big data-driven value creation opportunities.

The organizations that not only survive, but also thrive, during these data upheavals are those that embrace data and analytics as a core organizational capability. These organizations develop an insatiable appetite for data, treating it as an asset to be hoarded, not a business cost to be avoided. Such organizations manage analytics as intellectual property to be captured, nurtured, and sometimes even legally protected.

This book is for just such organizations. It provides a guide containing techniques, tools, and methodologies for feeding that insatiable appetite for data, to build comprehensive data management and analytics capabilities, and to make the necessary organizational adjustments and investments to leverage insights about your customers, products, and operations to optimize key business processes and uncover new monetization opportunities.

1 The Big Data Business Opportunity

Every now and then, new sources of data emerge that hold the potential to transform how organizations drive, or derive, business value. In the 1980s, we saw point-of-sale (POS) scanner data change the balance of power between consumer package goods (CPG) manufacturers like Procter & Gamble, Unilever, Frito Lay, and Kraft—and retailers like Walmart, Tesco, and Vons. The advent of detailed sources of data about product sales, soon coupled with customer loyalty data, provided retailers with unique insights about product sales, customer buying patterns, and overall market trends that previously were not available to any player in the CPG-to-retail value chain. The new data sources literally changed the business models of many companies.

Then in the late 1990s, web clicks became the new knowledge currency, enabling online merchants to gain significant competitive advantage over their brick-and-mortar counterparts. The detailed insights buried in the web logs gave online merchants new insights into product sales and customer purchase behaviors, and gave online retailers the ability to manipulate the user experience to influence (through capabilities like recommendation engines) customers' purchase choices and the contents of their electronic shopping carts. Again, companies had to change their business models to survive.

Today, we are in the midst of yet another data-driven business revolution. New sources of social media, mobile, and sensor or machine-generated data hold the potential to rewire an organization's value creation processes. Social media data provide insights into customer interests, passions, affiliations, and associations that can be used to optimize your customer engagement processes (from customer acquisition, activation, maturation, up-sell/cross-sell, retention, through advocacy development). Machine or sensor-generated data provide real-time data feeds at the most granular level of detail that enable predictive maintenance, product performance recommendations, and network optimization. In addition, mobile devices enable location-based insights and drive real-time customer engagement that allow brick-and-mortar retailers to compete directly with online retailers in providing an improved, more engaging customer shopping experience.

The massive volumes (terabytes to petabytes), diversity, and complexity of the data are straining the capabilities of existing technology stacks. Traditional data warehouse and business intelligence architectures were not designed to handle petabytes of structured and unstructured data in real-time. This has resulted in the following challenges to both IT and business organizations:

- Rigid business intelligence, data warehouse, and data management architectures are impeding the business from identifying and exploiting fleeting, short-lived business opportunities.
- Retrospective reporting using aggregated data in batches can't leverage new analytic capabilities to develop predictive recommendations that guide business decisions.
- Social, mobile, or machine-generated data insights are not available in a timely manner in a world where the real-time customer experience is becoming the norm.
- Data aggregation and sampling destroys valuable nuances in the data that are key to uncovering new customer, product, operational, and market insights.

This blitz of new data has necessitated and driven technology innovation, much of it being powered by open source initiatives at digital media companies like Google (Big Table), Yahoo! (Hadoop), and Facebook (Hive and HBase), as well as universities (like Stanford, UC Irvine, and MIT). All of these big data developments hold the potential to paralyze businesses if they wait until the technology dust settles before moving forward. For those that wait, only bad things can happen:

- Competitors innovate more quickly and are able to realize compelling cost structure advantages.
- Profits and margins degenerate because competitors are able to identify, capture, and retain the most valuable customers.
- Market share declines result from not being able to get the right products to market at the right time for the right customers.
- Missed business opportunities occur because competitors have real-time listening devices rolling up real-time customer sentiment, product performance problems, and immediately-available monetization opportunities.

The time to move is now, because the risks of not moving can be devastating.

The Business Transformation Imperative

The big data movement is fueling a business transformation. Companies that are embracing big data as business transformational are moving from a retrospective, rearview mirror view of the business that uses partial slices of aggregated or sampled data in batch to monitor the business to a forward-looking, predictive view of operations that leverages all available data—including structured and unstructured data that may sit outside the four walls of the organization—in real-time to optimize business performance (see Table 1-1).

Table 1-1: Big data is about business transformation.

Today's Decision Making	Big Data Decision Making
"Rearview Mirror" hindsight	"Forward looking" recommendations
Less than 10% of available data	Exploit all data from diverse sources
Batch, incomplete, disjointed	Real-time, correlated, governed
Business Monitoring	Business Optimization

Think of this as the advent of the real-time, predictive enterprise!

In the end, it's all about the data. Insight-hungry organizations are liberating the data that is buried deep inside their transactional and operational systems, and integrating that data with data that resides outside the organization's four walls (such as social media, mobile, service providers, and publicly available data). These organizations are discovering that data—and the key insights buried inside the data—has the power to transform how organizations understand their customers, partners, suppliers, products, operations, and markets. In the process, leading organizations are transforming their thinking on data, transitioning from treating data as an operational cost to be minimized to a mentality that nurtures data as a strategic asset that needs to be acquired, cleansed, transformed, enriched, and analyzed to yield actionable insights. Bottom-line: companies are seeking ways to acquire even more data that they can leverage throughout the organization's value creation processes.

Walmart Case Study

Data can transform both companies and industries. Walmart is famous for their use of data to transform their business model.

> *The cornerstone of his [Sam Walton's] company's success ultimately lay in selling goods at the lowest possible price, something he was able to do by pushing aside the middlemen and directly haggling with manufacturers to bring costs down. The idea to "buy it low, stack it high, and sell it cheap" became a sustainable business model largely because Walton, at the behest of David Glass, his eventual successor,* **heavily invested in software that could track consumer behavior in real time from the bar codes read at Walmart's checkout counters.**

> *He shared the real-time data with suppliers to create partnerships that allowed Walmart to exert significant pressure on manufacturers to improve their productivity and become ever more efficient. As Walmart's influence grew, so did its power to nearly dictate the price, volume, delivery, packaging, and quality of many of its suppliers' products. The upshot: Walton flipped the supplier-retailer relationship upside down.*[1]

Walmart up-ended the balance of power in the CPG-to-retailer value chain. Before they had access to detailed POS scanner data, the CPG manufacturers (such as Procter & Gamble, Unilever, Kimberley Clark, and General Mills,) dictated to the retailers how much product they would be allowed to sell, at what prices, and using what promotions. But with access to customer insights that could be gleaned from POS data, the retailers were now in a position where they knew more about their customers' behaviors—what products they bought, what prices they were willing to pay, what promotions worked the most effectively, and what products they tended to buy in the same market basket. Add to this information the advent of the customer loyalty card, and the retailers knew in detail what products at what prices under what promotions appealed to which customers. Soon, the retailers were dictating terms to the CPG manufacturers—how much product they wanted to sell (demand-based forecasting), at what prices (yield and price optimization), and what promotions they wanted (promotional effectiveness). Some of these retailers even went one step further and figured out how to monetize their POS data by selling it back to the CPG manufacturers. For example, Walmart provides a data service to their CPG manufacturer partners, called Retail Link, which provides sales and inventory data on the manufacturer's products sold through Walmart.

Across almost all organizations, we are seeing multitudes of examples where data coupled with advanced analytics can transform key organizational business processes, such as:

---

[1] "The 12 greatest entrepreneurs of our time" Fortune/CNN Money (http://money.cnn.com/galleries/2012/news/companies/1203/gallery.greatest-entrepreneurs.fortune/12.html)

- **Procurement:** Identify which suppliers are most cost-effective in delivering products on-time and without damages.
- **Product Development:** Uncover product usage insights to speed product development processes and improve new product launch effectiveness.
- **Manufacturing:** Flag machinery and process variances that might be indicators of quality problems.
- **Distribution:** Quantify optimal inventory levels and optimize supply chain activities based on external factors such as weather, holidays, and economic conditions.
- **Marketing:** Identify which marketing promotions and campaigns are most effective in driving customer traffic, engagement, and sales, or use attribution analysis to optimize marketing mixes given marketing goals, customer behaviors, and channel behaviors.
- **Pricing and Yield Management:** Optimize prices for "perishable" goods such as groceries, airline seats, concert tickets and fashion merchandise.
- **Merchandising:** Optimize merchandise markdown based on current buying patterns, inventory levels, and product interest insights gleaned from social media data.
- **Sales:** Optimize sales resource assignments, product mix, commissions modeling, and account assignments.
- **Store Operations:** Optimize inventory levels given predicted buying patterns coupled with local demographic, weather, and events data.
- **Human Resources:** Identify the characteristics and behaviors of your most successful and effective employees.

The Big Data Business Model Maturity Index

Customers often ask me:

- How far can big data take us from a business perspective?
- What could the ultimate endpoint look like?
- How do I compare to others with respect to my organization's adoption of big data as a business enabler?
- How far can I push big data to power—or even transform—my value creation processes?

To help address these types of questions, I've created the Big Data Business Model Maturity Index. This index provides a benchmark against which organizations can measure themselves as they look at what big data-enabled opportunities may lay ahead. Organizations can use this index to:

- Get an idea of where they stand with respect to exploiting big data and advanced analytics to power their value creation processes and business models (their current state).
- Identify where they want to be in the future (their desired state).

Organizations are moving at different paces with respect to how they are adopting big data and advanced analytics to create competitive advantages for themselves. Some organizations are moving very cautiously because they are unclear where and how to start, and which of the bevy of new technology innovations they need to deploy in order to start their big data journeys. Others are moving at a more aggressive pace to integrate big data and advanced analytics into their existing business processes in order to improve their organizational decision-making capabilities.

However, a select few are looking well beyond just improving their existing business processes with big data. These organizations are aggressively looking to identify and exploit new data monetization opportunities. That is, they are seeking out business opportunities where they can either sell their data (coupled with analytic insights) to others, integrate advanced analytics into their products to create "intelligent" products, or leverage the insights from big data to transform their customer relationships and customer experience.

Let's use the Big Data Business Model Maturity Index depicted in Figure 1-1 as a framework against which you can not only measure where your organization stands today, but also get some ideas on how far you can push the big data opportunity within your organization.

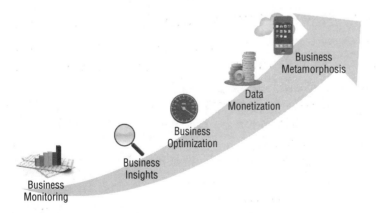

Figure 1-1: Big Data Business Model Maturity Index

Business Monitoring

In the *Business Monitoring* phase, you deploy Business Intelligence (BI) and traditional data warehouse capabilities to monitor, or report on, on-going business performance. Sometimes called *business performance management,* business monitoring uses basic analytics to flag under- or over-performing areas of the business, and automates sending alerts with pertinent information to concerned parties whenever such a situation occurs. The Business Monitoring phase leverages the following basic analytics to identify areas of the business requiring more investigation:

- Trending, such as time series, moving averages, or seasonality
- Comparisons to previous periods (weeks, months, etc.), events, or campaigns (for example, a back-to-school campaign)
- Benchmarks against previous periods, previous campaigns, and industry benchmarks
- Indices such as brand development, customer satisfaction, product performance, and financials
- Shares, such as market share, share of voice, and share of wallet

The Business Monitoring phase is a great starting point for your big data journey as you have already gone through the process—via your data warehousing and BI investments—of identifying your key business processes and capturing the KPIs, dimensions, metrics, reports, and dashboards that support those key business processes.

Business Insights

The *Business Insights* phase takes business monitoring to the next step by leveraging new unstructured data sources with advanced statistics, predictive analytics, and data mining, coupled with real-time data feeds, to identify material, significant, and actionable business insights that can be integrated into your key business processes. This phase looks to integrate those business insights back into the existing operational and management systems. Think of it as "intelligent" dashboards, where instead of just presenting tables of data and graphs, the application goes one step further to actually uncover material and relevant insights that are buried in the detailed data. The application can then make specific, actionable recommendations, calling out an observation on a particular area of the business where specific actions can be taken to improve business performance. One client called this phase the "Tell me what I need to know" phase. Examples include:

- In marketing, uncovering observations that certain in-flight campaign activities or marketing treatments are more effective than others, coupled with specific recommendations as to how much marketing spend to shift to the more effective activities.
- In manufacturing, uncovering observations that certain production machines are operating outside of the bounds of their control charts (for example, upper limits or lower limits), coupled with a prioritized maintenance schedule with replacement part recommendations for each problem machine.
- In customer support, uncovering observations that certain gold card members' purchase and engagement activities have dropped below a certain threshold of normal activity, with a recommendation to e-mail them a discount coupon.

The following steps will transition your organization from the business monitoring to the business insights stage.

1. Invest the time to understand how users are using existing reports and dashboards to identify problems and opportunities. Check for situations where users are printing reports and making notes to the side of the reports. Find situations where users are downloading the reports into Excel or Access and capture what these users are doing with the data once they have it downloaded. Understanding what your users are doing with the existing reports and downloads is "gold" in identifying the areas where advanced analytics and real-time data can impact the business.

2. Understand how downstream constituents—those users that are the consumers of the analysis being done in Step 1—are using and making decisions based on the analysis. Ask, "What are these constituents doing with the results of the analysis? What actions are they trying to take? What decisions are they trying to make given the results of the analysis?"

3. Launch a prototype or pilot project that provides the opportunity to integrate detailed transactional data and new unstructured data sources with real-time data feeds and predictive analytics to automatically uncover potential problems and opportunities buried in the data (Insights), and generate actionable recommendations.

Business Optimization

The *Business Optimization* phase is the level of business maturity where organizations use embedded analytics to automatically optimize parts of their business operations. To many organizations, this is the Holy Grail where they can turn over certain parts of their business operations to analytic-powered applications that automatically optimize the selected business activities. Business optimization examples include:

- Marketing spend allocation based on in-flight campaign or promotion performance
- Resource scheduling based on purchase history, buying behaviors, and local weather and events
- Distribution and inventory optimization given current and predicted buying patterns, coupled with local demographic, weather, and events data
- Product pricing based on current buying patterns, inventory levels, and product interest insights gleaned from social media data
- Algorithmic trading in financial services

The following steps will transition your organization from the Business Insights phase to the Business Optimization phase:

1. The Business Insights phase resulted in a list of areas where you are already developing and delivering recommendations. Use this as the starting point in assembling the list of areas that are candidates for optimization. Evaluate these business insights recommendations based on the business or financial impact, feasibility of success, and their relative recommendation performance or effectiveness.
2. For each of the optimization candidates, identify the supporting business questions and decision-making process (the analytic process). You will also need to identify the required data sources and timing/latency of data feeds (depending on decision-making frequency and latency), the analytic modeling requirements, and the operational system and user experience requirements.
3. Finally, conduct "Proof of Value" or develop a prototype of your top optimization candidates to verify the business case, the financials (return on investment—ROI), and analytics performance.

You should also consider the creation of a formal analytics governance process that enables human subject matter experts to audit and evaluate the effectiveness and relevance of the resulting optimization models on a regular basis. As any good data scientist will tell you, the minute you build your analytic model it is obsolete due to changes in the real-world environment around it.

Data Monetization

The *Data Monetization* phase is where organizations are looking to leverage big data for net new revenue opportunities. While not an exhaustive list, this includes initiatives related to:

- Packaging customer, product, and marketing insights for sale to other organizations
- Integrating analytics directly into their products to create "intelligent" products
- Leveraging actionable insights and personalized recommendations based on customer behaviors and tendencies to upscale their customer relationships and dramatically rethink their "customer experience"

An example of the first type of initiative could be a smartphone app where data and insights about customer behaviors, product performance, and market trends are sold to marketers and manufacturers. For example, MapMyRun (www.MapMyRun.com) could package the customer usage insights from their smartphone application with audience and product insights for sale to sports apparel manufacturers, sporting goods retailers, insurance companies, and healthcare providers.

An example of the second type of initiative could be companies that leverage new big data sources (sensor data or user click/selection behaviors) with advanced analytics to create "intelligent" products, such as:

- Cars that learn your driving patterns and behaviors and use the data to adjust driver controls, seats, mirrors, brake pedals, dashboard displays, and other items to match your driving style.
- Televisions and DVRs that learn what types of shows and movies you like and use the data to search across the different cable channels to find and automatically record similar shows for you.
- Ovens that learn how you like certain foods cooked and uses the data to cook them in that manner automatically, and also include recommendations for other foods and cooking methods that others like you enjoy.

An example of the third type of initiative could be companies that leverage action-able insights and recommendations to "up-level" their customer relationships and dramatically rethink their customer's experience, such as:

■ Small, medium business (SMB) merchant dashboards from online market-places that compare current and in-bound inventory levels with customer buying patterns to make merchandising and pricing recommendations
■ Investor dashboards that assess investment goals, current income levels, and current financial portfolios to make specific asset allocation recommendations

The following steps will be useful in helping transition to the Data Monetization phase.

1. Identify your target customers and their desired solutions. Focus on identify-ing solutions that improve customers' business performance and help them make money. As part of that process, you will need to detail out the personas of the economic decision-makers. Invest time shadowing these decision-mak-ers to understand what decisions they are trying to make, how frequently, and in what situations. Spend the time to gather details of what they are trying to accomplish, versus focusing on trying to understand what they are doing.

2. Inventory your current data assets. Capture what data you currently have. Also, identify what data you could have with a little more effort. This will require you to look at how the source data is being captured, to explore additional instrumentation strategies to capture even more data, and explore external sources of data that, when combined with your internal data, yields new insights on your customers, products, operations, and markets.

3. Determine the analytics, data enrichment, and data transformation processes necessary to transform your data assets into your targeted customers' desired solutions. This should include identifying:

■ The business questions and business decisions that your targeted per-sonas are trying to ask and answer
■ The advanced analytics (algorithms, models), data augmentation, transformation, and enrichment processes necessary to create solutions that address your targeted persona's business questions and business decisions
■ Your targeted persona's user experience requirements, including their existing work environments and how you can leverage new mobile and data visualization capabilities to improve that user experience

Business Metamorphosis

The *Business Metamorphosis* phase is the ultimate goal for organizations that want to leverage the insights they are capturing about their customers' usage patterns, product performance behaviors, and overall market trends to transform their business models into new services in new markets. For example:

- Energy companies moving into the home energy optimization business by recommending when to replace appliances (based on predictive maintenance) and even recommending which brands to buy based on the performance of different appliances compared to customer usage patterns, local weather, and environmental conditions, such as local water conditions and energy costs.
- Farm equipment manufacturers transforming into farming optimization businesses by understanding crop performance given weather and soil conditions, and making seed, fertilizer, pesticide, and irrigation recommendations.
- Retailers moving into the shopping optimization business by recommending specific products given a customer's current buying patterns compared with others like them, including recommendations for products that may not even reside within their stores.
- Airlines moving into the "Travel Delight" business of not only offering discounts on air travel based on customers' travel behaviors and preferences, but also proactively finding and recommending deals on hotels, rental cars, limos, sporting or musical events, and local sites, shows, and shopping in the areas that they are visiting.

In order to make the move into the Business Metamorphosis phase, organizations need to think about moving away from a product-centric business model to a more platform- or ecosystem-centric business model.

Let's drill into this phase by starting with a history lesson. The North American video game console market was in a massive recession in 1985. Revenues that had peaked at $3.2 billion in 1983, fell to $100 million by 1985—a drop of almost 97 percent. The crash almost destroyed the then-fledgling industry and led to the bankruptcy of several companies, including Atari. Many business analysts doubted the long-term viability of the video game console industry.

There were several reasons for the crash. First, the hardware manufacturers had lost exclusive control of their platforms' supply of games, and consequently lost the ability to ensure that the toy stores were never overstocked with products. But the main culprit was the saturation of the market with low-quality games. Poor quality games, such as *Chase the Chuck Wagon* (about dogs eating food, bankrolled by the dog food company Purina), drove customers away from the industry.

The industry was revitalized in 1987 with the success of the Nintendo Entertainment System (NES). To ensure ecosystem success, Nintendo instituted strict measures to ensure high-quality games through licensing restrictions, maintained strict control of industry-wide game inventory, and implemented a security lockout system that only allowed certified games to work on the Nintendo platform. In the process, Nintendo ensured that third-party developers had a ready and profitable market.

As organizations contemplate the potential of big data to transform their business models, they need to start by understanding how they can leverage big data and the resulting analytic insights to transform the organization from a product-centric business model into a platform-centric business model. Much like the Nintendo lesson, you accomplish this by creating a marketplace that enables others—like app developers, partners, VARs, and third party solution providers—to make money off of your platform.

Let's build out the previous example of an energy company moving into the home energy optimization business. The company could capture home energy and appliance usage patterns that could be turned into insights and recommendations. For example, with the home energy usage information, the company could recommend when consumers should run their high energy appliances, like washers and dryers, to minimize energy costs. The energy company could go one step further and offer a service that automatically manages when the washer, dryer, and other high-energy appliances run—such as running the washer and dryer at 3:00 a.m. when energy prices are lower.

With all of the usage information, the company is also in a good position to predict when certain appliances might need maintenance (for example, monitoring their usage patterns using Six Sigma control charts to flag out-of-bounds performance problems). The energy company could make preventive maintenance recommendations to the homeowner, and even include the names of three to four local service dealers and their respective Yelp ratings.

But wait, there's more! With all of the product performance and maintenance data, the energy company is also in an ideal position to recommend which appliances are the best given the customer's usage patterns and local energy costs. They could become the *Consumer Reports* for appliances and other home and business equipment by recommending which brands to buy based on the performance of different appliances as compared to their customers' usage patterns, local weather, environmental conditions, and energy costs.

Finally, the energy company could package all of the product performance data and associated maintenance insights and sell the data and analytic insights back to the manufacturers who might want to know how their products perform within certain usage scenarios and versus key competitors.

In this scenario, there are more application and service opportunities than any single vendor can reasonably supply. That opens the door to transform to a platform-centric business model that creates a platform or ecosystem that enables third party developers to deliver products and services on that platform. And, of course, this puts the platform provider in a position to take a small piece of the "action" in the process, such as subscription fees, rental fees, transaction fees, and referral fees.

Much like the lessons of Nintendo with their third-party video games, and Apple and Google with their respective apps stores, creating such a platform not only benefits your customers who are getting access to a wider variety of high-value apps and services in a more timely manner, it also benefits the platform provider by creating a high level of customer dependency on your platform (for example, by increasing the switching costs).

Companies that try to do all of this on their own will eventually falter because they'll struggle to keep up with the speed and innovation of smaller, hungrier organizations that can spot and act on a market opportunity more quickly. Instead of trying to compete with the smaller, hungrier companies, enable such companies by giving them a platform on which they can quickly and profitability build, market, and support their apps and solutions.

So how does your company make the business metamorphosis from a product to a platform or ecosystem company? Three steps are typically involved:

1. Invest the time researching and shadowing your customers to understand their desired solutions. Focus on what the customer is trying to accomplish, not what they are doing. Think more broadly about their holistic needs, such as:

   - Feeding the family, not just cooking, buying groceries, and going to restaurants
   - Personal transportation, not just buying or leasing cars, scheduling maintenance, and filling the car with gas
   - Personal entertainment, not just going to the theater, buying DVDs, or downloading movies

2. Understand the potential ecosystem players (e.g., developers) and how they could make money off of your platform. Meet with potential ecosystem players to brainstorm and prioritize their different data monetization opportunities to:

   - Clarify, validate, and flush out the ecosystem players' business case
   - Identify the platform requirements that allow the ecosystem players to easily instrument, capture, analyze, and act on insights about their customers' usage patterns and product performance

3. As the platform provider, focus product development, marketing, and partnering efforts on ensuring that the platform:

  ■ Is easy to develop on and seamlessly supports app developer marketing, sales, service, and support (for example, app fixes, new product releases, addition of new services)

  ■ Is scalable and reliable with respect to availability, reliability, extensibility, data storage, and analytic processing power

  ■ Has all the tools, data processing, analytic capabilities (such as recommendation engines), and mobile capabilities to support modern application development

  ■ Simplifies how qualified third parties make money with respect to contracts, terms and conditions, and payments and collections

  ■ Enables developers to easily capture and analyze customer usage and product performance data in order to improve their customers' user experience and help the developers optimize their business operations (for example, pricing, promotion, and inventory management)

This step includes creating user experience mockups and prototypes so that you can understand *exactly* how successfully and seamlessly customers are able to interact with the platform (for example, which interface processes cause users the most problems, or where do users spend an unusual amount of time). Mockups are ideal for web- or smartphone-based applications, but don't be afraid to experiment with different interfaces that have different sets of test customers to improve the user experience. Companies like Facebook have used live experimentation to iterate quickly in improving their user experience. Heavily instrument or tag every engagement point of the user experience so that you can see the usage patterns and potential bottlenecks and points of frustration that the users might have in interacting with the interface.

As your organization advances up the big data business model maturity index, you will see three key cultural or organizational changes:

■ Data is becoming a corporate asset to exploit, not a cost of business to be minimized. Your organization starts to realize that data has value, and the more data you have at the most granular levels of detail, the more insights you will be able to tease out of the data.

■ Analytics and the supporting analytic algorithms and analytic models are becoming organizational intellectual property that need to be managed, nurtured, and sometimes even protected legally. The models that profile, segment, and acquire your customers, the models that you measure campaign or healthcare treatment effectiveness, the models that you use to predict equipment maintenance—all of these are potential differentiators in the marketplace that can be exploited for differentiated business value and may need to be legally protected.

■ Your organization becomes more comfortable making decisions based on the data and analytics. The business users and business management become more confident in the data and begin trusting what the data is telling them about their business. The need to rely solely on the organization's HiPPO (Highest Paid Person's Opinion) gives way to an organizational culture that values making decisions based on what the data and the analytics are showing.

Big Data Business Model Maturity Observations

The first observation is that the first three phases of the Big Data Business Model Maturity Index are internally focused—optimizing an organization's internal business processes, as highlighted in Figure 1-2. This part of the maturity index leverages an organization's data warehouse and business intelligence investments, especially the key performance indicators, data transformation algorithms, data models, and reports and dashboards around the organization's key business processes. There are four big data capabilities that organizations can leverage to enhance their existing internal business processes as part of the maturity process:

■ Mine all the transactional data at the lowest levels of detail much of which is not being analyzed today due to data warehousing costs. We call this the organizational "dark" data.

■ Integrate unstructured data with detailed structured (transactional) data to provide new metrics and new dimensions against which to monitor and optimize key business processes.

■ Leverage real-time (or low-latency) data feeds to accelerate the organization's ability to identify and act upon business and market opportunities in a timely manner.

■ Integrate predictive analytics into your key business processes to uncover insights buried in the massive volumes of detailed structured and unstructured data. (Note: having business users slice and dice the data to uncover insights worked fine when dealing with gigabytes of data, but doesn't work when dealing with terabytes and petabytes of data.)

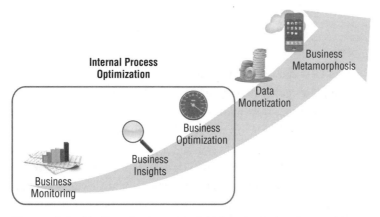

Figure 1-2: Big Data Business Model Maturity Index: Internal Process Optimization

The second observation is that the last two phases of the Big Data Business Model Maturity Index are externally focused—creating new monetization opportunities based upon the customer, product, and market insights gleaned from the first three phases of the maturity index, as highlighted in Figure 1-3. This is the part of the big data journey that catches most organizations' attention; the opportunity to leverage the insights gathered through the optimization of their internal business processes to create new monetization opportunities. We call this area of the Big Data Business Model Maturity Index the four Ms of big data: *Make Me More Money*!

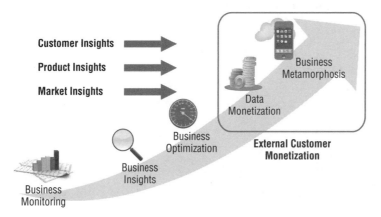

Figure 1-3: Big Data Business Model Maturity Index: External Customer Monetization

Summary

This chapter introduced you to the business drivers behind the big data movement. I talked about the bevy of new data sources available covering structured, semi-structured (for example, log files generated by sensors), and unstructured (e.g., text documents, social media postings, physician comments, service logs, consumer comments) data. I also discussed the growing sources of publicly available data that reside outside the four walls of an organization.

This chapter also briefly covered why traditional data warehousing and business intelligence technologies are struggling with the data volumes, the wide variety of new unstructured data sources and the high-velocity data that shrinks the latency between when a data event occurs and when that data is available for analysis and actions.

Probably most importantly, you learned how leading organizations are leveraging big data to transform their businesses—moving from a retrospective view of the business with partial chunks of data in batch to monitor their business performance, to an environment that integrates predictive analytics with real-time data feeds that leverage all available data in order to optimize the business.

Finally, you were introduced to the concept of the Big Data Business Model Maturity Index as a vehicle for helping your organization identify where they are today, and map out where they could be with respect to leveraging big data to uncover new monetization and business metamorphosis opportunities. Several "How To" guides were included in this chapter to help your organization move from one phase to the next in the maturity index.

2

Big Data History Lesson

hapter 1 hinted at how retail point-of-sale (POS) scanner data caused a big data revolution that transformed the Consumer Package Goods (CPG) and retail industries in the late 1980s and 1990s. Let's spend a bit more time on that event, as there are some valuable lessons to be learned that apply to today's big data revolution.

Consumer Package Goods and Retail Industry Pre-1988

In the 1970s and early 1980s, CPG manufacturers such as Procter & Gamble, Unilever, Colgate-Palmolive, Kraft, and General Mills, to name but a few, and large grocery, drug, and mass merchandise retailers made their marketing decisions based on bi-monthly Nielson store audit data. That is, Nielsen would send people into a sample of stores (in only about 12 cities across the United States) to conduct physical audits—to count how much product was on the shelf, the price of the product, how much linear footage the product had across the front of the shelf, product sales within that store, and other data. Nielsen would aggregate this information by product category in order to calculate market share by volume and revenue, share of shelf space, etc. The results of the audits were then delivered every two months to the retailers and CPG manufacturers, usually in booklet format. CPG manufacturers could also request the data in tape format, but the data volumes were easily in the megabyte range.

So a company like Procter & Gamble would use this data for their Crest brand toothpaste, combined with their own internal orders and shipments data, to compare their sales to other toothpaste brands in the dentifrice product category. The Crest brand team would use this data to plan, execute, and measure their marketing strategies including promotional spending, new product introductions, and pricing decisions.

NOTE Not only was Crest's data and analysis only available bimonthly, but the audit books were delivered several weeks after the close of the audit period due to the data cleansing, alignment, and analytics that Nielsen had to do to ensure accuracy and consistency of the data. Needless to say, it could be two to three months after a marketing campaign ended before the manufacturer had any idea how successful their campaign had been in driving incremental revenue, unit sales, and market share increases.

Then in the late 1980s, Information Resources Inc. (IRI) introduced their Infoscan product, which combined retail POS scanner systems with barcodes (universal product codes—UPC) to revolutionize the CPG-to-retail value chain process. Data volumes jumped from megabytes to gigabytes and soon to terabytes of retail sales data. Existing mainframe-based executive information systems (EIS) broke under the data volumes, which necessitated a next generation of data processing capabilities as represented by client-server architectures, and data platforms such as Britton-Lee, Red Brick, Teradata, Sybase IQ, and Informix. This also saw the birth of the Business Intelligence (BI) software industry (e.g., Brio, Cognos, Microstrategy, Business Objects), as many early BI companies can trace their origins to the late 1980s Procter & Gamble-led "decision support" projects.

So data volumes jumped dramatically, breaking existing technology platforms and necessitating a next generation of data platforms and analytic capabilities. Sound familiar? But the most interesting thing wasn't the jump in data volumes that necessitated a new generation of data processing and analytic capabilities. The most interesting and relevant aspect of the scanner POS revolution was how companies like Procter & Gamble, Frito Lay, Tesco, and Walmart were able to leverage this new source of data and new technology innovations to create completely new business applications—business applications that previously were impossible to create. Much like what was discussed in Chapter 1 about moving to the Business Insights and Business Optimization phases of the Big Data Business Model Maturity Index, these new business applications leveraged the detailed POS data and new data management and analytic innovations to create new application categories such as:

- **Demand-based Forecasting**, where CPG manufacturers could create and update their product forecasts in near real-time based on what products were selling in the retail outlets for that current week. This was a major breakthrough for companies that sold products that were considered staples—products with relatively consistent consumption, such as toilet paper, toothpaste, soap, detergent, and most food products.

- **Supply Chain Optimization**, where detailed product sales data at the UPC level, combined with up-to-date inventory data (at each distribution center, at each store, and on order), allowed retailers and CPG manufacturers to drive excess inventory, holding, and distribution costs out of the supply chain. The savings in reduced capital required to maintain the supply chain was significant in itself, not to mention savings in other areas such as spoilage, shrinkage and unnecessary labor, distribution center and transportation costs.

- **Trade Promotion Effectiveness**, where CPG manufacturers could more quickly quantify what trade promotions were working most effectively with which retailers, and do this analysis in a more timely manner to actually impact current trade promotion programs.

- **Market Basket Analysis**, where retailers could gain intimate knowledge of what products sold together to what customers at what times of year. This insight could be used to not only change how retailers would lay out their stores, but also put the retailer in a superior position to inform the CPG manufacturers of the optimal cross-product category promotional opportunities.

- **Category Management** was an entirely new concept championed by leading CPG manufacturers. Much like how brand management had revolutionized the management and marketing of brands just a couple of decades earlier, Category Management allowed CPG manufacturers to re-apply many of the brand management concepts, but at a product category level (for example, heavy duty detergents, toilet paper, diapers, or dentifrice) in order to drive overall category demand, efficiencies, and profitability. This created a common language where retailers and CPG manufacturers could collaborate to drive overall category sales and profitability. The "category champion," which was the title or role given to the CPG manufacturer, was responsible for the management of the retailer's in-store product category including pricing, replenishment, promotions, and inventory.

- **Price and Yield Optimization**, where organizations are determining optimal product prices—at the individual store and seasonality levels—by combining real-time sales data with historical sales (demand), product sales seasonality trends and available inventory (on-hand and on-order). For example, retailers know that they can charge more for the same products in high tourist areas (e.g., Sanibel Island) than they can charge in normal residential areas due to the degree of price insensitivity of vacationing shoppers.

- **Markdown Management**, where retailers integrated POS historical sales data for seasonal or short-lived fashion products to intelligently reduce product prices based on current inventory data and product demand trends to optimize the product or merchandise markdown management process. For example, grocery, mass merchandiser, and drug chain retail outlets used the POS data with advanced analytics to decide when and how much to mark down Easter, Christmas, Valentine's Day, and other holiday-specific items. And mass merchandisers and department stores used the POS data with advanced analytics to decide when and how much to mark down seasonal items such as swimsuits, parkas, winter boots, and fashion items.

■ **Customer Loyalty Programs** were to me the biggest innovation. Retailers suddenly had the opportunity to introduce customer loyalty cards that could be scanned at the time of product purchase in exchange for product discounts and reward programs. Just check your billfold or purse to see how many of these programs you personally belong to. (For me that would include Starbucks, Safeway, Walgreens, Sports Authority, and Foot Locker, just to name a few.) This allowed retailers to tie specific product and market basket purchases to the demographics of their individual shoppers. The potential profiling, targeting, and segmentation possibilities were almost endless, and provided a potentially rich source of insights that retailers could use to better market, sell and service to their most important customers.

Figure 2-1 summarizes the key takeaways with respect to how point-of-sale scanner data drove the CPG-Retail industry transformation.

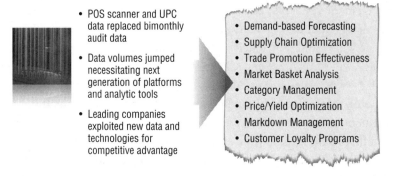

- POS scanner and UPC data replaced bimonthly audit data

- Data volumes jumped necessitating next generation of platforms and analytic tools

- Leading companies exploited new data and technologies for competitive advantage

- Demand-based Forecasting
- Supply Chain Optimization
- Trade Promotion Effectiveness
- Market Basket Analysis
- Category Management
- Price/Yield Optimization
- Markdown Management
- Customer Loyalty Programs

Figure 2-1: Big Data History Lesson: 1980s CPG and retail industries transitioned from bimonthly audit data to POS scanner data

The combination of new data sources and technology innovations also led to new data monetization opportunities (the Data Monetization phase of our Big Data Business Model Maturity Index), such as Walmart's Retail Link that provided detailed product sales information to Walmart's CPG manufacturing and distribution partners. The creation of a platform or ecosystem from which partners and other value-added developers can deliver new services, capabilities and applications is the start of moving into the Business Metamorphosis phase discussed in Chapter 1.

Ultimately, this more detailed, high-velocity data changed the balance of power in the CPG-Retail industry. Prior to the advent of POS scanner data, CPG manufacturers leveraged their superior knowledge of their customers' buying behaviors (painstakingly gathered through countless focus groups, surveys, and primary research) to dictate sales and payment terms to the retailers. However, courtesy of the POS scanner data and resulting customer and product insights, the retailers suddenly knew more about their customers' buying behaviors, price and promotional sensitivities, and product and market basket preferences. Retailers were able to leverage these superior customer and product insights to dictate product pricing, promotional, and delivery terms to the CPG manufacturers.

Lessons Learned and Applicability to Today's Big Data Movement

The introduction of retail scanner POS systems created new sources of data that required new technologies to manage the data, and new analytic software to analyze the data. But the real competitive advantages came from organizations that exploited the new sources of data and new technology innovations to derive—or drive—new sources of business differentiation, competitive advantage, and monetization.

How does the POS scanner data history lesson apply to the big data movement today? First, new massive volumes of high-velocity structured and unstructured data—both inside and outside of the organization—are breaking traditional data management tools and platforms, and data and analytic modeling techniques. Data sources such as web logs, social media posts, doctor's notes, service comments, research papers, and machine and sensor-generated data are creating data volumes that have some leading organizations already working with petabytes of data, and planning for the inevitable introduction of zettabytes of data. Traditional data management and data warehousing platforms were never designed for the volume, velocity, or complexity of these types of data sources.

Next, new tools must be developed to exploit this tsunami of new data sources. Digital media companies such as Google, Yahoo!, and Facebook—companies whose primary value proposition is built around managing huge data volumes and consequently monetizing that data—have had to develop new technologies to manage and analyze this data, creating technologies such as Hadoop, MapReduce, Pig, Hive, and HBase.

Ultimately, though, the winners will be those organizations that exploit the new data sources, coupled with advancements in data management and advanced analytic technologies, to upgrade or enrich existing business processes or create new business applications that provide unique sources of competitive advantage and business differentiation. Much like how Procter & Gamble (with Category Management), Walmart (with Supply Chain Optimization), and Tesco (with Customer Loyalty Programs) gained competitive advantage from new data sources and new technology innovations, companies today should be focused on determining where data and technology innovation can rewire their existing value creation processes to create new value for their customers, and uncover new sources of revenue and profits for their organizations.

Summary

This chapter covered the history lesson from the late 1980s, where retail POS scanner data created an earlier "big data" revolution. POS scanner data volumes quickly jumped from megabytes to gigabytes and ultimately to terabytes of data, replacing the bimonthly store audit data that had previously been used to make marketing, promotional, product, pricing, and placement decisions.

You reviewed how the volume, diversity, and velocity of this POS data broke existing data management and analytical technologies. EIS analytic software that ran on mainframes could not handle the volume of data, which gave birth to new data processing technologies such as specialized data management platforms (Red Brick, Teradata, Britton Lee, Sybase IQ) and new analytic software packages (Brio, Cognos, Microstrategy, Business Objects).

Finally, the chapter covered how the ultimate winners were those companies who were able to create new analytics-driven business applications, such as category management and demand-based forecasting. Suddenly, retailers with immediate access to POS scanner data coupled with customer loyalty data knew more about customer shopping behaviors and product preferences that they used to change the industry balance of power and dictate terms to CPG manufacturers with respect to pricing, packaging, promotion, and in-store product placement.

3

Business Impact of Big Data

Organizations are starting to realize that big data is more about business transformation than IT transformation. Big data is allowing companies to answer questions they could not previously answer, and make more timely decisions at a finer level of fidelity than before, yielding new insights that can deliver business differentiation and new operational efficiencies. Let's take a look at an example of how big data is transforming how we look at business.

For decades, leading organizations have been exploiting new data sources, plus new technologies, for business differentiation and competitive advantage. And for the most part, the questions that the business users are trying to ask, and answer, with these data sources and new technologies really haven't changed:

- Who are my most valuable customers?
- What are my most important products?
- What are my most successful campaigns?
- What are my best performing channels?
- What are my most effective employees?

The more I thought about these "simple" questions, the more I realized just how "not simple" these questions really were. Because of the new insights available from new big data sources, companies are able to take these types of "simple" questions to the next level of sophistication and understanding.

Let's look at the most valuable customer question. When you ask who your most valuable customers are, do you mean largest by revenue (which is how many companies today still define their most valuable customers)? Or do you mean the most profitable customers, contemplating more aspects of the customer engagement including marketing and sales costs, cost to service, returns, and payment history (which is how some of the more advanced companies think today)? Or by adding social media into the mix, do you now mean your most influential customers and the financial value associated with their circle of friends?

Companies are learning that their most profitable customers may not actually be their most valuable customers because of the net influencer or advocacy effect. Advocates can have significant influence and persuasive effect on a larger community of customers, and the profitability of the "baskets" associated with that community of customers. Same with the most important product question, which retailers have understood for quite a while (think loss leaders like milk that drive store traffic even though they don't drive much in the form of profits), and consumer goods manufacturers understand as well (think category strategies and the use of flanking products to protect their premium-priced core products).

Those nebulous and hard-to-define words, like valuable, important, and successful, allow the business users to move beyond just financial measures and to consider the entirety of the contributions those customers, products, and campaigns make to the business. It is the basis for a more engaging business discussion about what data sources could be critical in defining "valuable" and what analytic models could be used to quantify "valuable." It's the basis for a wonderful conversation that you can have with your business users about defining those valuable, important, and successful words in light of what big data and advanced analytics can bring to the table.

Big Data Impacts: The Questions Business Users Can Answer

Big data has changed the nuances for defining and quantifying terms such as valuable, important, and successful. It is these nuances that fuel the insights that are the source of competitive advantage and business differentiation. New big data sources, plus new advanced analytic capabilities, enable higher fidelity answers to these questions, and provide a more complete understanding of your customers, products, and operations that can drive business impact across various business functions, such as:

- Merchandising to identify which marketing promotions and campaigns are the most effective in driving store or site traffic and sales.
- Marketing to optimize prices for perishable goods such as groceries, airline seats, and fashion merchandise.
- Sales to optimize the allocation of scarce sales resources against the best sales opportunities and most important or highest potential accounts.
- Procurement to identify which suppliers are most cost-effective in delivering high-quality products in a predictable and timely manner.

- Manufacturing to flag machine performance and process variances that might be indicators of manufacturing, processing, or quality problems.
- Human Resources to identify the characteristics and behaviors of your most successful and effective employees.

Managing Using the Right Metrics

Since baseball is one of my loves in life, and in honor of the enlightening book, *Moneyball: The Art of Winning an Unfair Game,* by Michael Lewis (Norton, 2004), I thought it was only appropriate to discuss how the pursuit and identification of the right metrics has not only changed how the game of baseball is managed, but has the same potential impact on how you manage your business.

In 2004, Lewis wrote the book *Moneyball*, which chronicled how the Oakland A's and Billy Beane, their general manager, were using new data and metrics in order to determine the value of any particular player. The A's were unique at that time in the use of *sabermetrics*, which is the application of statistical analysis to baseball data in order to evaluate and compare the performance of individual players. The results were that the A's had a demonstrable competitive advantage in determining how much to pay any particular player playing any specific position, especially in the costly era of free agency.

As a result, the A's enjoyed a significant cost advantage in what they were paying for wins versus a team like the Yankees. The comparison is shown in Figure 3-1.

	Salaries ($M)		Wins		Cost per Win ($M)		
	A's	Yankees	A's	Yankees	A's	Yankees	A's % of Yankees
2005	$55.4	$208.3	88	95	$0.63	$2.19	29%
2004	$59.4	$184.2	91	101	$0.65	$1.82	36%
2003	$50.3	$152.7	96	101	$0.52	$1.51	35%
2002	$40.0	$125.9	103	103	$0.39	$1.22	32%
2001	$33.8	$112.3	102	95	$0.33	$1.18	28%
2000	$32.1	$88.1	91	87	$0.35	$1.01	35%
	$271.0	$871.5	571	582	$0.47	$1.50	32%

Yankee Batting KPIs:	**A's Batting KPIs:**
• Batting average • RBIs • Fielding percentage • Steals	• On-base percentage • Slugging percentage

Figure 3-1: Payroll cost per win: Athletics versus Yankees

Unfortunately for Billy Beane and the Oakland A's, other teams (most notably the Boston Red Sox) copied this model and reduced the competitive advantage that the A's briefly enjoyed. But that's the nature of a competitive business isn't it, whether it's in sports, retail, banking, entertainment, telecommunications, or healthcare.

So how does one survive in a world where competitive advantage via analytics can be so short-lived? By constantly innovating, thinking differently, and looking at new sources of data and analytic tools to bring to light those significant, material, and actionable insights that can differentiate your business from that of your competitors.

One of the challenges with metrics is that eventually folks learn how to game the metrics for their own advantage. Sticking with our baseball scenario, let's take the Fielding Percentage metric as an example. The Fielding Percentage metric is calculated as the total number of plays (chances minus errors) divided by the number of total chances. Some players have learned that one of the ways to improve their Fielding Percentage is to stop trying to field balls that are outside of their fielding comfort zone. If you don't try hard for the ball, there can't be an error assessed. While that might be good for the individual's performance numbers, it is obviously less than ideal for the team who wants all of their players trying to make plays in the field. Let's see how that works.

Let's say that an outfielder has 1,000 fielding chances, and makes 20 errors out of those 1,000 fielding chances for a Fielding Percentage of 98 percent (see Figure 3-2). Now, if the fielder doesn't try to field the 100 hardest opportunities (resulting in only 900 Fielding Chances), he will likely cut down significantly on the number of errors (let's say, eliminating 10 errors) resulting in an increased Fielding Percentage of 98.9 percent.

- Example: Fielding Percentage
  - Fielding percentage: total plays (chances minus errors) divided by the number of total chances

$$\text{Fielding Percentage} = \frac{\text{(Chances} - \text{Errors)}}{\text{Number of total chances}}$$

- However, a player can "game" the system by not trying to catch difficult chances

	Tries	Doesn't Try
Number of Chances	1000	900
Errors (example)	20	10
Fielding Percentage	98.0%	98.9%

By not trying to catch the 100 most difficult chances, the player commits an estimated 10 fewer errors and improves their field percentage

- Note: In 2011 for Center Fielders, the #1 and #11 top-fielding percentages were separated by 0.9 basis points (100.0% to 99.1%).

Figure 3-2: Picking the wrong metrics can incentivize the wrong behaviors

While the 0.9 basis-point difference (98.9 minus 98.0) between the two efforts may not seem significant, suffice it to say that the difference between the #1 center fielder in Major League Baseball in 2011 and the #11 center fielder was only 0.9 basis points. The difference probably means millions of dollars to their playing contract.

So the bottom line is that some players have figured out that they will perform better by only trying to field those opportunities within their comfort zone. Not the sort of behavior that leads to very many World Series appearances.

So how does the world of big data change this measure? Baseball stadiums have installed video cameras throughout the stadium to get a better idea as to actual game dynamics. One of the benefits of these cameras is a new set of metrics that are better predictors of players' performance.

For example, video cameras now can measure how much many feet a particular fielder can cover within a certain period of time in fielding their position. Ultimately, this will lead to the creation of an Effective Fielding Range metric which measures how much of the playing field the fielder can cover, and how effectively they cover the playing field (see Figure 3-3). This metric will allow baseball management to value players differently because Effective Fielding Range is a much better predictor of fielding performance than the traditional Fielding Percentage.

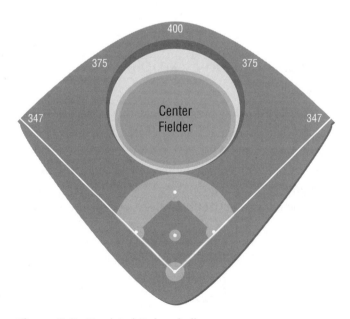

Figure 3-3: Big data hits baseball

As illustrated in the figure, the Center Fielder is very efficient in covering the outfield going left, right, or forward (indicated by the green coverage area), but is less efficient going backwards (indicated by the yellow and red coverage areas).

Much like the world of baseball, organizations must be constantly vigilant in search of metrics that are better predictors of business performance. The new data sources and analytic capabilities enabled by big data hold huge potential to be the first mover in uncovering those significant, measurable, and actionable insights that can lead to competitive advantage—on the baseball field or in the corporate battlefields.

Data Monetization Opportunities

Data monetization is certainly the holy grail of the big data discussion: How do I leverage my vast wealth of customer, product, and operational insights to provide new revenue-generating products and services, enhance product performance and the product experience, and create a more compelling and "sticky" customer relationship?

But how does one even start thinking about this data monetization discussion? Let me take a data monetization example from the digital media world and present a process that other industries can use to uncover and capitalize on potential data monetization opportunities.

Digital Media Data Monetization Example

Digital media companies like Yahoo!, Google, Facebook, and Twitter have worked to master the data monetization process. They must because their entire business model is built on monetizing data. These companies work with bytes to create services, unlike most other companies who work with atoms to build physical products like shoes, tractors, houses, and burrito bowls with double chicken and guacamole.

So what process do these digital media companies go through to identify how to monetize their data assets? The data monetization process starts with two key understandings:

1. Who are my target customers (targeted personas) and what business solutions do they need for which they are willing to pay?
2. What data assets do I have (or could I have)?

Once you have a solid understanding of these two questions, then you are in a position to start the data monetization process.

Digital Media Data Assets and Understanding Target Users

First, digital media companies need to identify and really (and I mean really!) understand their target customers—that is, who is making the million dollar marketing and campaign decisions, and what information and insights do they need to make those decisions? Digital media companies target the following three customers or personas: Media Planners and Buyers, Campaign Managers, and Digital Media Executives. These digital media decision-makers buy the following "solutions":

- Audiences, such as soccer moms, country squires, gray power, and weekend warriors
- Inventory (like sports, finance, news, and entertainment) available on certain days and times of days
- Results or measures, such as Cost per Thousands (CPM) of impressions, Cost Per Acquisition (CPA), product sales, or conversions (where conversions could include getting a visitor to share their e-mail address, request a quote, or schedule a reservation)

For each of these targeted personas, the digital media company needs to understand what questions they are trying to answer, what decisions they are trying to make, under what circumstances they are making these decisions, and within what sort of environment or user experience they are typically working when they have to answer their questions and make their decisions.

Next, digital media companies assess the breadth, depth, and quality of their data assets, including:

- Visitors and their associated demographic, psycho-demographic, and behavioral insights
- Properties and the type of content and advertising real estate (e.g., full banner, pop-under, skyscraper, leaderboard, half-page) that is provided on properties (like Yahoo! Finance, Yahoo! Sports, or Yahoo! Entertainment)
- Activities that visitors perform on those properties (for example, they viewed a display impression, moused over a display ad, clicked a display ad, entered a keyword search) including how often, how recent, and in what sequence

This data assessment process should also include what additional data could be captured through data acquisition, as well as through more robust instrumentation and experimentation techniques.

Data Monetization Transformations and Enrichments

The key challenge is then to transform, augment, enrich, and repackage the data assets into the solutions that the target digital media customers want to buy. For example, digital media companies instrument or set up their sites and tag their visitors (via cookies) to capture visitors' web site and search activities in order to determine or ascertain additional visitor insights, including:

- Geographic information such as ZIP code, city, state, and country
- Demographic information such as gender, age, income, social class, religion, race, and family lifecycle
- Psycho-demographic information such as lifestyle, personality, and values
- Behavioral attributes such as consumption behaviors, lifestyles, patterns of buying and using, patterns of spending money and time, and similar factors
- Product categories of interest (Schmarzo likes Chipotle, Starbucks, the Cubs and the Giants, and all things basketball)
- Social influences such as interests, passions, associations, and affiliations

With this information in hand, the digital media company needs the data processing capacity and advanced analytical skills to profile, segment, and package those visitors into the audiences that advertisers and advertising agencies want to buy.

This data transformation, augmentation, and enrichment process is then repeated in converting properties into inventory, visitor activities into digital treatments, and campaigns into results such as sales and conversions (see Table 3-1).

NOTE The table below has been organized with step 1 at the far right, as it represents the end solutions that we are trying to deliver. Step 2 is on the far left as it represents the key data assets, which will go through step 3 to be transformed and enriched into our targeted solutions.

Table 3-1: Data Monetization Example—Digital Media Company

Step 2: Assess Data Assets	Step 3: Identifying Transformation, Enrichment, and Analytic Requirements	Step 1: Define Digital Advertiser Solutions
Visitor	Demographics Insights	Audiences
	Psycho-Demographics Insights	What audiences am I reaching?
	Behavioral Insights	Who is my most engaged audience?
	Social and Mobile Insights	What similar audiences could I target?

Step 2: Assess Data Assets	Step 3: Identifying Transformation, Enrichment, and Analytic Requirements	Step 1: Define Digital Advertiser Solutions
Properties (Sites)	Product categories (Sports, Finance) Audiences Premium vs. Remnant	Inventory What inventories are most effective? What product categories are most effective? What other product categories should I use?
Web Activities	Impressions Clicks Keyword Searches Social Posts and Activities Mobile Tracking	Marketing Treatments What marketing treatments are most effective? What are minimum frequency/recency levels? What is the optimal sequencing of treatments?
Campaigns	Instrumentation Analytics (Attribution, Audience Insights, Benchmarking) Optimizations and Predictions Recommendations User Experience	Sales/Conversions/CPM Will I achieve campaign objectives (predict)? What will be the impact if I re-allocate spending? What recommended changes will improve performance? How can I optimize inflight cross-media spending?

Based on this digital media example, here are the steps that your company needs to go through in order to better understand how to monetize your data assets.

1. Identify your target customers and their desired solutions (solution capabilities and required insights) in order to optimize their performance and simplify their jobs. Identify and profile the target business customers or personas for those solutions, and internalize how those customers will use that solution within their existing work environment. Quantify the business value of those solutions, and document the business questions the users need to answer and business decisions the business users need to make as part of the desired solution.

2. Inventory and assess your data assets; that is, identify the most important and valuable "nouns" of your business. Understand what additional data could be

gathered to enrich your data asset base via data acquisition and a more robust instrumentation and experimentation strategy.

3. Understand the aggregation, transformation, cleansing, alignment, data enrichment, and analytic processes necessary to transform your data assets into business solutions. Document what insights and analytics you can package that meets your customers' needs for a solution that optimizes business performance and simplifies their jobs. Identify the data enrichment and analytic processes necessary to transform data into actionable insights and understand how those insights manifest themselves within the customers' user experience.

There are numerous opportunities for organizations to improve product performance, enhance product design and development, preempt product failure, and enhance the overall user (shopper, driver, patient, subscriber, member) experience. More and more, the data and the resulting insights teased out of the data will become a key component, and potentially a differentiator, in the products and services that companies provide.

Summary

This chapter covered how asking the right questions is one of the key starting points in your big data journey. You learned how big data has changed the nuances for defining and quantifying terms, such as *valuable, important*, and *successful*, and saw some examples of how big data is helping various business functions ask the right questions at a finer level of fidelity.

Then I reviewed how big data is enabling organizations to identify new measures and metrics that are better predictors of business performance. I discussed the impact that the book *Moneyball* and the world of sabermetrics has had on helping baseball teams, particularly the Oakland A's, exploit a superior understanding of the "right" metrics to optimize baseball success on the baseball field. I also provided an example of how big data is taking the world of baseball analytics to the next level of predictive excellence with new insights about baseball player performance that are better predictors of in-game success.

The chapter concluded with a discussion on how you can monetize your data assets. I reviewed how your organization can leverage data assets to deliver new revenue opportunities and a more compelling, differentiated business relationship through superior customer, product, and market insights. I used the world of digital media marketing as an example and provided a "How To" framework to help your organization explore data monetization opportunities by understanding your target customers (personas) and their desired solutions, understanding your data assets, and by identifying the data transformation, enrichment, and analytic processes necessary to transform your data assets into business solutions.

4 Organizational Impact of Big Data

One of the more significant impacts of big data is the organizational change or transformation necessary to support and exploit the big data opportunity. Old roles will need to be redefined and new roles introduced, creating both opportunities and anxiety for individuals and organizations alike. The purpose of this chapter is to highlight the likely extent of these organizational changes and to prepare existing data warehouse and business intelligence professionals for the new career opportunities before them.

Business intelligence (BI) and data science (involving advanced statistics, predictive analytics, data engineering, programming, and data visualization) have very different roles and require different skills and approaches. One does not replace the other. In fact, the two very much complement each other, one playing off the strengths and focus of the other. BI traditionally has focused on understanding key business processes at a detailed enough level so that metrics, reports, dashboards, alerts, and some basic analytics (trending, comparisons) can be built that support those key business processes. To support these key business processes, the BI analyst has gone through the process of capturing the roles, responsibilities, and expectations of the business users, identifying key performance indicators against which the performance of those business processes will be measured, and capturing, aggregating, aligning, cleansing, and making available the data (at the necessary levels of granularity and frequency) to support the monitoring of those business processes. The understanding of these business processes is the linkage point between the worlds of BI and data science.

Figure 4-1 and Table 4-1 present useful visual presentations of the complementary worlds of BI and data science. BI is typically thought of as being retrospective—providing a rearview mirror view of the business, focusing on what happened and why (hindsight). Data science is typically thought of as being forward thinking—providing a forward-looking, windshield view of the business, predicting what is going to happen (foresight) and uncovering hidden nuggets buried in the vast volumes of structured and unstructured data (insights). However, many BI implementations do include some basic analytical analysis such as time series analysis, comparisons to previous periods, and "what if" modeling, in order to help the business make forward-looking decisions such as: What price should I charge? What customers should I target? How many clerks am I going to need?

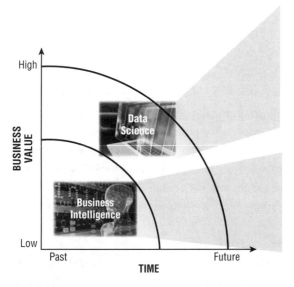

Figure 4-1: Evolution of the analytic process

Table 4-1: Business Intelligence versus Data Science

Typical Techniques and Data Types	Common Questions
Business Intelligence	
Standard and ad hoc reporting, dashboards, alerts, queries, details on demand basic statistical analysis	What happened last quarter?
	How many did we sell?
Structured data, traditional sources, manageable data sets	Where is the problem? In what situations does the problem occur?
Data Science	
Optimization, predictive modeling, forecasting, recommendations, advanced statistical analysis	What if...?
	What's the optimal scenario for our business?
Structured/unstructured data, any types of sources, very large data sets	What will happen next? What if these trends continue? Why is this happening?

One of the biggest differences between the BI analyst and data scientist is the environment in which they work. BI specialists tend to work within a highly structured data warehouse environment. A data warehouse environment is typically production driven, with highly managed service level agreements (SLAs) in order to ensure timely generation of management reports and dashboards. It takes a yeoman's effort to add a new data source (often this effort is measured in months) or to get the approval to keep more granular data and/or more history in the data warehouse.

The data scientist, however, creates a separate analytic "sandbox" in which to load whatever data they can get their hands on (both internal and external data sources) and at whatever level of granularity and history they need. Once within this environment, the data scientist is free to do with it whatever they wish (for example, data profiling, data transformations, creation of new composite metrics, and analytic model development, testing and refinement). The data scientist needs an environment where they can easily explore the data without concerns about impacting the performance of the production data warehouse and BI systems that generate the management reports and dashboards. Table 4-2 presents a clear summary of the inherently different types of work that the BI analyst is doing versus the type of work that the data scientist is doing.

Table 4-2: BI Analyst versus Data Scientist Responsibilities

Area	BI Analyst	Data Scientist
Focus	Reports, KPIs, trends	Patterns, correlations, models
Process	Static, comparative	Exploratory, experimentation, visual
Data sources	Pre-planned, added slowly	Chosen on the fly, on-demand
Transformation	Up front, carefully planned	ELT, on-demand, in-database, enrichment
Data quality	Single version of truth	Tolerant of "good enough"; probabilities
Data model	Logical/relational/formal	Conceptual/semantic/informal
Results	Report what happened	Predict what will happen
Analysis	Hindsight	Forecast, foresight, insight

Data Analytics Lifecycle

Successful big data organizations continuously uncover and publish new customer, product, operational, and market insights about the business. Consequently, these organizations need to develop a comprehensive process that not only defines how these insights will be uncovered and published, but clearly defines the roles, responsibilities, and expectations of all key stakeholders including the business users, data warehouse managers, BI analysts, and data scientists. Let's use the analytics lifecycle to gain an understanding of how these different stakeholders collaborate (see Figure 4-2).

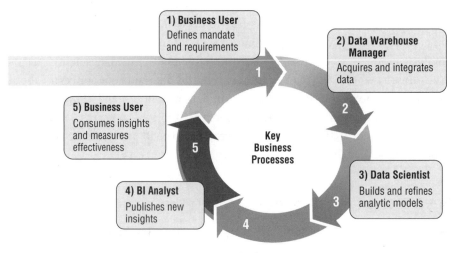

Figure 4-2: The analytics lifecycle

This flowchart highlights the key responsibilities for each major stakeholder:

- The *business user* (which also includes the business analyst) is responsible for defining their key business processes, and identifying the metrics and key performance indicators against which those business processes will be measured. The business users are the ones who understand what questions they are trying to answer and what decisions they are trying to make. The business users are the ones who are trying to leverage the available data and insights to answer those questions and make those decisions.
- The *data warehouse manager* (or DBA in some cases) is responsible for defining, developing, and managing the data platform. The traditional tools of choice for this stakeholder has historically been data warehouses, data marts, and operational data stores. However, new technology innovations are enabling the

data warehouse manager to broaden their role by considering new technologies such as Hadoop, in-memory computing, and data federation. These new data platforms support both structured and unstructured data and provide access to data located both inside the organization as well as select data sources that exist outside the four walls of the organization. These modern data platforms also support the ability to ingest and analyze real-time data feeds and enable the "trickle feeding" of data into the data platform.

■ The *data scientist* is responsible for mining the organization's data—structured and unstructured data that is both internal and external of the organization—to uncover new insights about the business. Data scientists are data hoarders, seeking out new sources of data that can fuel the analytic insights that power the organization's key business processes. The data scientist needs a work environment (analytic sandbox) where they are free to store, transform, enrich, integrate, interrogate, and visualize the data in search of valuable relationships and insights buried across the different data sources. The data scientist needs an environment that allows them to build, test, and refine data models rapidly—measured in minutes and hours, not days, and weeks—and embraces the "fail enough times" approach that gives the data scientist confidence in the quality of the analytic models. "Fail enough times" refers to the point in the analytic model development and testing process where the data scientist has "failed" enough times in testing other variables and algorithms that they feel confident that the resulting model is the best analytic model.

■ The *BI analyst* is responsible for identifying, managing, presenting and publishing the key metrics and key performance indicators against which the business users will monitor and measure business success. BI analysts develop the reports and dashboards that the business users use to run the business and provide the "channel" for publishing analytic insights through those reports and dashboards to the business users. This is where the real-time, predictive enterprise vision comes to fruition.

■ And finally, the analytic process circles back to the business users who use the resulting reports, dashboards, and analytic insights to run their business. It is the business users, and the effectiveness of the decisions that they make, who ultimately determine the effectiveness of the work done by the data warehouse manager, data scientist, and BI analyst. Finally, the results of the decisions that the business users make can be captured and used to fuel the next iteration of the analytic lifecycle.

The exact nature of the roles, responsibilities, and expectations of these different stakeholders will vary from organization to organization, and even project to project. Some business users may be more comfortable with statistics and predictive analytics, and may seek to do some of the analytic work themselves. Same with the BI analysts who are looking to broaden their skill sets with advanced analytics and data visualization skills.

It should be noted that the roles and responsibilities for each stakeholder are centered on a targeted key business processes. The roles and responsibilities might very well change for each key business process, depending upon the skills, capabilities, and areas of interest of the different stakeholders. So view this analytics lifecycle more as a framework to provide some level of guidance for organizational collaboration, versus a fixed set of roles and responsibilities that ignores the individual skills and interests of the different stakeholders.

Data Scientist Roles and Responsibilities

Our next step is to dive more deeply into the specific roles and responsibilities of the data scientist. The data scientist lifecycle depicted in Figure 4-3 provides a high-level overview of the data scientist discovery and analysis process. It highlights the highly iterative nature of the data scientist's work, with many of the steps being repeated in order to ensure the data scientist is using the "right" analytic model to find the "right" insights. Let's take a look at the specific tasks and skills required for each of the data scientist lifecycle steps.

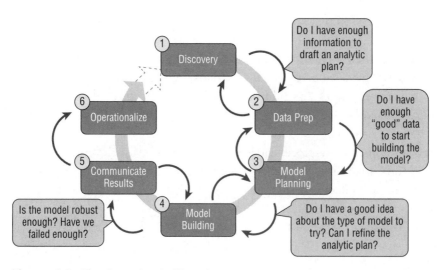

Figure 4-3: The data scientist lifecycle

Discovery

Discovery focuses on the following data scientist activities:

- Gaining a detailed understanding of the business process and the business domain. This includes identifying the key metrics and key performance indicators against which the business users will measure success.
- Capturing the most important business questions and business decisions that the business users are trying to answer in support of the targeted business process. This also should include the frequency and optimal timeliness of those answers and decisions.
- Assessing available resources (for example, people skills, data management and analytic tools, and data sources) and going through the process of framing the business problem as an analytic hypothesis. This is also the stage where the data scientist builds the initial analytics development plan that will be used to guide and document the resulting analytic models and insights.

It should be noted that understanding into which production or operational environments the analytic insights need to be published is something that should be identified in the analytics development plan. This information will be critical as the data scientist identifies in the plan where to "operationalize" the analytic insights and models.

This is an ideal opportunity for tight collaboration with the BI analyst who likely has already defined the metrics and processes required to support the business initiative. The BI analyst will have a good understanding of the business users' decision-making environment and requirements that can jumpstart the data scientist's analytics development plan.

Data Preparation

Data preparation focuses on the following data scientist activities:

- Provisioning an analytic workspace, or an analytic sandbox, where the data scientist can work free of the constraints of a production data warehouse environment. Ideally, the analytic environment is set up such that the data scientist can self-provision as much data space and analytic horsepower as required and can adjust those requirements throughout the analysis process.
- Acquiring, cleansing, aligning, and analyzing the data. This includes using data visualization techniques and tools to gain an understanding of the data, identifying (and eliminating as necessary) outliers in the data and assessing gaps in the data to determine the overall data quality; ascertaining if the data is "good enough."

- Transforming and enriching the data. The data scientist will look to use analytic techniques, such as logarithmic and wavelet transformations, to address potential skewing in the data. The data scientist will also look to use data enrichment techniques to create new composite metrics such as frequency (how often?), recency (how recent?), and sequencing (in what order?). The data scientist will make use of standard tools like SQL and Java, as well as both commercial and open source extract, transform, load (ETL) tools to transform the data.

At the end of this step, the data scientist needs to feel comfortable enough with the quality and richness of the data to advance to the next stage of the analytics development process.

There are several opportunities for the data scientist to collaborate with the data warehouse team, especially the ETL team, to understand what ETL and transformation tools are already being used and available, and what transformation code or algorithms have already been written.

Model Planning

Model planning focuses on the following activities:

- Determining the different analytic models, methods, techniques and workflows to explore as part of the analytic model development. The data scientist might already believe that they know which analytic models and techniques are most appropriate, but it is always a good idea to have a plan to test at least one other to ensure that the opportunity to build a more predictive model is not missed.
- Determine correlation and collinearity between variables in order to select key variables to be used in the model development. As much as possible, the data scientist wants to quantify the cause-and-effect variables. Practical judgment will have to be used by the data scientist, and this may even be a good opportunity to re-engage with the BI analyst and the business users to ensure that the variables being selected "make sense." Remember, correlation does not guarantee causation, so care must be taken in selecting variables that not only make sense, but are also variables that can be measured going forward.

Model Building

Model building focuses on the following activities:

- Massaging the data sets for testing, training, and production. New transformation techniques may have to be tested to see if the quality, reliability, and predictive capabilities of the data can be improved.

- Assessing the viability and reliability of data to use in the predictive models. Judgment calls will have to be made on quality and reliability of the data—is the data "good enough" to be used in developing the analytic models. Again, different transformation techniques may have to be tested to see if the quality of the data can be improved.
- Finally, developing, testing, and refining the analytic models. Testing is conducted to see which variables and analytic models deliver the highest quality, most predictive and actionable analytic insights.

This is a highly iterative step where massaging of the data, assessing the reliability of the data, and determining the quality and predictive powers of the analytic model will be fine-tuned several times. And this is not a straight-line process. The data scientist will fail several times in testing different variables and modeling techniques before settling into the "right" one. This is the "art" of the analytic model development process where the data scientist, as an artisan, is "playing" with the data to see what predictive capabilities can be teased out of the data and the analytic model. This is the fun stage!

Communicate Results

The *communicate results* step is where the data scientist focuses on the following activities:

- Ascertaining the quality and reliability of the analytic model and statistical significance, measurability, and actionability of the resulting analytic insights. The data scientist needs to ensure that the analytic process and model was successful and achieved the desired analytic objectives of the project.
- Developing the charts and graphics to communicate the analytic model insights, results, and recommendations. It is critical that the business stakeholders—the business users, business analysts, and the BI analysts—understand and "buy into" the resulting analytic insights. If the business stakeholders do not have confidence in the results, then your work will have been for naught.

The BI analysts are natural allies in this part of the data science lifecycle. The BI analysts have a solid understanding of what to present to their business users and how to present it. They understand the business users' work environment and the presentation tools, current operational reporting, and management dashboards in which the analytic results are likely to be published. The BI analysts can help to ensure that the resulting analytics are presented in an actionable manner or format to the business stakeholders.

Operationalize

The *operationalize* step is where the data scientist focuses on the following activities:

- Delivering the final recommendations, reports, briefings, code, and technical documents.
- Optionally, running a pilot or analytic lab to verify the business case, and the financial return on investment (ROI) and the analytic lift.
- Implementing the analytic models in the production and operational environments. This involves working with the application and production teams to determine how best to surface the analytic results and insights. The application and production teams can help determine how to "productionize" the analytic models so they run on a regular, scheduled basis, something that should have been covered in the analytics development plan.
- Integrating analytic scores into management dashboards and operational reporting systems, such as call centers, sales systems, procurement systems, and financial systems.

The operationalization stage is another area where collaboration between the data scientist and the BI analysts should be invaluable. Many BI analysts already have experience integrating reports and dashboards into the operational systems, as well as establishing centers of excellence to propagate analytic learning and skills across the organization.

New Organizational Roles

Big data is causing organizations to rethink how they manage, grow and protect their new, big data assets—analytic insights, analytic models, and data. Let's review three new and critical roles that need to be added to the big data team.

User Experience Team

Leading big data organizations are starting to realize that if you can't present the results of your big data analytics in a way that's intuitive and actionable to the business stakeholders, then why bother? These organizations are realizing that they need to have a user experience (UEX) team as part of the big data team.

When I was working at Yahoo!, I had the great fortunate to work with two very experienced user experience designers. They taught me the value of an actionable yet simple user interface (think Apple iPod simple). Web companies like Yahoo!, Amazon, and eBay were some of the first companies to understand the importance of the UEX. Soon other companies employed "user centric design" as a core differentiator in developing compelling and engaging products and services. We define user-centric design as:

User-centered design is a process in which the needs, wants, and limitations of end users of a product are given extensive attention at each stage of the design process. User-centered design can be characterized as a multi-stage problem solving process that not only requires designers to analyze and foresee how users are likely to use a product, but also to test the validity of their assumptions with regards to user behavior in real world tests with actual users.[1]

The UEX architects and designers taught me the importance of UEX tools and techniques such as:

- Personas to document and clearly understand the usage characteristics, decision-making processes, and the work environment within which the targeted users work.
- Storyboarding to capture the user experience requirements, navigational requirements, and usage patterns and flow on paper.
- Wireframes where the user experience requirements start taking life, especially with how to navigate around the interface to find the necessary information (for example, everything above the fold, nothing more than two clicks away).
- Flash mockups that let the target users interact with the mockups to identify UEX design flaws, navigation problems, and inaccurate usage assumptions.

New Senior Management Roles

Organizations are starting to realize that they need to treat their data and analytics as strategic corporate assets. This is leading to the creation of two new senior management roles: the chief data officer and the chief analytics officer. These two new roles will be involved in proactively managing the company's data assets and analytics intellectual property.

The *chief data officer* will be responsible for acquiring, storing, enriching, and leveraging the company's data assets. This role is likely to be filled by people with an economics or finance background as they look at ways to put economic value on the data that they have and want to acquire. The chief data officer role could cover the following responsibilities:

- **Data inventory:** Many organizations don't even know what data sources they have, so this role would be responsible for inventorying data (looking for unnecessary and redundant data purchases) and determining how that data is being used (to determine if the organization should continue to capture the data). This role would also have the critical responsibility for identifying and placing value on external data sources that could be acquired.

[1] http://en.wikipedia.org/wiki/User-centered_design

- **Data economic valuation:** Establish a framework around which to determine the economic value of the organization's data, especially as companies look to acquire more external, partner, and third-party data.
- **Data monetization:** Establish a process to continuously evaluate the organization's data assets for monetization opportunities through improved decision-making, integrating data into physical products, or packaging data for sale to other organizations.
- **Instrumentation:** Develop strategies to determine how to use tags, beacons, and sensors across operational, web, and mobile platforms to capture additional customer, product, and operational data.
- **Data governance:** Develop and enforce (audit) a set of processes that ensures that important data assets are formally and consistently managed across the enterprise to ensure the appropriate level of data cleanliness and accuracy.

The *chief analytics officer* will be responsible for capturing and tracking the analytic models and resulting analytic insights that are developed and deployed throughout the organization. The ideal chief analytics officer probably has a law degree to legally protect the organization's analytical intellectual property (IP) including—data models, analytic models, and analytic algorithms. The chief analytics officer role could cover the following responsibilities:

- **Analytic assets:** Collaborate with the data science team to inventory analytic models and algorithms throughout the organization.
- **Analytics valuation:** Establish a framework and process for determining the financial value of the organization's analytic assets.
- **Intellectual property management:** Develop processes and manage a repository for the capture and sharing of organizational IP (check-in, check-out, versioning).
- **Patent applications:** Manage the patent application and tracking process for submitting patents to protect key organizational analytics IP.
- **Intellectual property protection:** Monitor industry analytics usage to identify potential IP violations, and then lead litigation efforts to stop or get licensing agreements for IP violations.
- **Intellectual property monetization:** Actively look for business partners and opportunities to sell or license organizational analytics IP.

We see organizations looking to expand the data science team and senior leadership positions to further exploit the competitive advantage offered by big data. The User Experience team is a powerful addition to the data science team, in that the team has a role that is singularly focused on ensuring that the right analytics are delivered to the right users at the right time in the most actionable and relevant way. And the chief data officer and chief analytics officer roles ensure that the data and analytics intellectual property assets are properly acquired, managed, packaged, and valued by the organization; and that there are roles on the CEO staff whose focus and success is defined by how well those assets are monetized.

Liberating Organizational Creativity

Ah, the anguish of not knowing the "right" answers. Organizations struggle with the process of determining the "right" answers, resulting in lots of wasted debates and divisive arguments regarding whose answers are more right. They even have a name for this debilitating process—analysis paralysis—where different sides of the argument bring forth their own factoids and antidotal observations to support the justification of their "right" answer. There is good news, however, as the concepts of experimentation and instrumentation can actually liberate organizations from this analysis paralysis by providing a way out—a way forward that leads to action versus just more debate, more frustrations, and more analysis paralysis.

For many organizations, the concepts of experimentation and instrumentation are a bit foreign. Internet companies (such as Yahoo!, Google, Facebook, Amazon) and direct marketing organizations have ingrained these two concepts into their analytics and customer engagement processes. They have leveraged the concepts of experimentation and instrumentation to free up the organizational thinking—to freely explore new ideas and test hunches—but in a scientific manner that results in solid evidence and new organizational learning.

Let's understand how your organization can embrace these same concepts as part of your big data strategy. Let's start by defining two key concepts:

- *Experimentation* is defined as the act, process, practice, or an instance of making experiments, where an experiment is a test, trial, or tentative procedure; an act or operation for the purpose of discovering something unknown or of testing a principle, supposition, etc.[2]
- *Instrumentation* is defined as the art and science of measurement and control of process variables within a production or manufacturing area.[3]

Taken together, these two concepts can liberate organizations that are suffering from analysis paralysis—struggling when they are not certain as to what decision to make (e.g., Should I increase prices 10 percent or decrease prices 10 percent? Should I use the purple ad or the red ad? Should I offer promotion A or promotion B?).

[2] http://dictionary.reference.com/browse/experiment
[3] http://en.wikipedia.org/wiki/Instrumentation

Taken together, these two concepts can power the creative "what if" thinking process that is critical as an organization looks to embrace big data. The "what if" analytics cycle can advance the organization's understanding of the business potential of new sources of structured and unstructured data, located both internally and externally to the organization, coupled with advanced analytics and data science methodologies (see Figure 4-4 below).

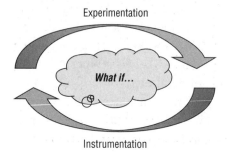

Figure 4-4: "What if" experimentation cycle

This "what if" analytic cycle *empowers* organizations to freely debate different ideas without having to worry about which ideas are right ahead of time. Consequently, organizations can embrace an environment of experimentation to encourage the free flow of new ideas. Organizations can let the results tell them which ideas are "right" and not let the most persuasive debater or most senior person make that determination. It *empowers* the organization to challenge conventional thinking, and *empowers* creative thinking that can surface potentially worthy ideas. You no longer do have to spend endless hours or days debating whose idea is right. Instead, put the ideas to the test and let the data tell you!

Let's walk through an example of how one would leverage the "what if" analytics cycle:

1. Develop a hypothesis or theory that you want to test. For example, I believe that my target audience will respond more favorably to Offer A, while my colleague believes that Offer B is more attractive to our target audience.

2. Create an experiment (for example, a test environment with corresponding test cases) that can prove or disprove the hypothesis. We also want to identify the metrics against which we will measure the test results (for example, click-through rate, store traffic, sales). In this example, we would create tests

for three test cases: Offer A, Offer B, and a Control Group. We would employ sampling techniques to select our test and control members, and ensure that other potential variables are held constant during the test (for example, same time of day, same audience characteristics, same channel, timeframe, etc.).

3. Instrument all test cases in order to measure the results of the test. In this example, we'd want to ensure that each of the three test cases were appropriately "tagged" and that we were capturing all the relevant data to determine who responded to which offers, who didn't respond, and what were the results of their responses.

4. Execute the tests. For our example, we would determine the start and stop dates for the tests, run the tests, capture relevant data and results, and then conclude the test.

5. Quantify the test results. We would look at the results of the tests, examine who clicked on what ads, determine the final results, and declare a winner. And more importantly, we would then move onto the next test.

The beauty of an organization that embraces the "what if" experimentation and instrumentation analytic cycle is to test both ideas, and then let the data tell us which one is right. The "what if" analytics cycle leverages experimentation and instrumentation to empower the organization to freely explore and test new ideas, and empowers organizations to get moving by not getting bogged down in analysis paralysis. In fact, big data is the anti-analysis paralysis by giving organizations the data, tools, and methodologies to test ideas, learn from those tests, and move on.

Summary

This chapter covered the organizational impact of big data, specifically the organizational impact of adding the data scientist to the organization's existing analytics lifecycle process. I laid out an analytic lifecycle where the roles, responsibilities, and expectations of each key stakeholder—business users, DBA/data warehouse managers, data scientists, and BI analysts—are clearly defined to ensure tighter collaboration against a targeted business process.

The chapter also dove deeply into the specific roles and responsibilities of the data scientist as part of the data science lifecycle. I described each of the key tasks within the different data science lifecycle stages, and also identified specific areas where close collaboration with the data warehouse, ETL, and BI teams could be beneficial to the data scientist.

Next, we covered new organizational roles that are being dictated by the needs and potential of big data. We discussed the importance of the user experience team, and that team's role with respect to the other members of the big data team. We also discussed new senior management roles—the chief data officer and the chief analytics officer—and the critical nature of those roles to capture, augment, preserve, and even legally protect the growing portfolio of corporate big data assets.

Finally, we covered the liberating effect of embracing a culture of experimentation—empowering organizational "what if" thinking—and how the concept of experimentation can free up the creative juices of both individuals and the organization as a whole.

5 Understanding Decision Theory

One interesting aspect of big data is how it is challenging the conventional thinking regarding how the non-analytical business user should be using analytics. An article by Chris Anderson titled "The End of Theory: The Data Deluge Makes the Scientific Method Obsolete" really got me thinking about not only the power of big data and advanced analytics, but more importantly what the combination of big data and advanced analytics might mean to the business user experience. The premise of the article was that the massive amounts of data were yielding insights about businesses without requiring the heavy statistical modeling typically needed when using sampled data sets. This is the quote that really intrigued me:

> *Google conquered the advertising world with nothing more than applied mathematics. It didn't pretend to know anything about the culture and conventions of advertising — it just assumed that better data, with better analytical tools, would win the day. And Google was right.*[1]

Google became the dominant player in an industry (advertising) without really knowing anything about that industry. Google achieved this role not by understanding and perfecting advertising techniques, but by applying analytics to massive, detailed data sources to identify what works *without having to worry about why it worked.*

Business Intelligence Challenge

That's the key "aha" moment that big data practitioners need to understand—that you can leverage these vast, detailed, and diverse data sets to yield *significant, material, and actionable insights* on your business processes. You don't necessarily

---

[1] http://www.wired.com/science/discoveries/magazine/16-07/pb_theory

have to apply statistical techniques to these massive data sets to understand *why* certain behaviors occur or why certain things happen because you are not dealing with samples, but instead are dealing with the complete population of data.

Business users, who by their very nature are not statistical analysis experts, have struggled to learn and integrate statistical analysis into their daily business processes. And business intelligence tools have failed to help business users make the transition from reporting to analytic insights and optimization because the tools were inadequate in helping users understand *why* something happened. Significant statistical training and handcrafting were required to help business users quantify cause and effect in order to build the models necessary to predict what to do next, and that was beyond their training and interest. As a result, the users' transition to a predictive, forward-looking view of their business fell into the "analytics chasm" (see Figure 5-1).

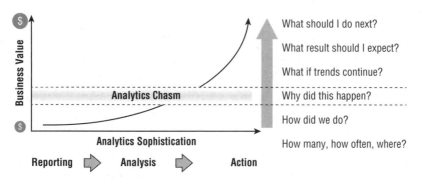

Figure 5-1: The analytics chasm

The analytics chasm is that area of data analysis where users are trying to apply statistical algorithms to their data in order to *quantify cause and effect*—identify the correlation between certain actions and resulting outcomes. The users hope that if they can quantify cause and effect, then they are in a better position to support the "what if" exploration process, predict what result they should expect from what actions, and uncover recommendations as to what they should do next to improve business performance.

However, trying to turn the average business user into a statistical specialist (the early version of a data scientist) failed in the early 2000s and it continues to fail today. The average business user's career aspiration is not to become a statistical expert or a data scientist. They are in the retail, medical, telecommunications, banking, or other industries because they like that industry, not because they want to master statistics or manage large data sets. The tools today are way too hard to make that process trivial. So what is one to do?

Big data provides the opportunity to mitigate the need to master statistical skills in order to understand why things happen. With the vast and diverse amounts of detailed data available and high-powered analytic tools, it's possible to identify what works *without having to worry about why it worked*. This can enable you to think differently about the user interface and the context and manner in which you present business insights to your users.

The Death of Why

Big data coupled with advanced analytics enables organizations to identify significant, material, and actionable insights buried in the data, *without having to understand why these insights occur*. This concept provides the foundation for an entirely different analytic process. Instead of presenting a seemingly endless series of reports and charts in a dashboard in the hope that users can slice and dice their way to discovering what's driving business performance, organizations can leverage predictive analytics to reverse the traditional analytic process and present to their business users only those insights which are important to their business. This is done by leveraging advanced analytics, new sources of detailed structured and unstructured data, and real-time data feeds to uncover and publish to the business users only those material and actionable insights buried in the data.

This insights-lead analytics process means that the user's analysis process can start with those material and actionable insights uncovered in the data, coupled with specific recommendations to improve business performance. This new analytic process can still support the data discovery and exploration processes by providing the ability for the business users to drill into the supporting details behind the insights. But this perspective turns the traditional analytic process on its head—instead of starting the analytic process with an overwhelming number of charts and tables in hopes that the user can manipulate the charts and tables to find something of interest, the "insights-lead analytics process" leads with specific insights into areas that might be impacting business performance (see Figure 5-2).

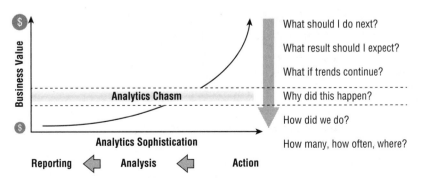

Figure 5-2: The death of why

Big Data User Interface Ramifications

This new insights-lead analytics process can enable an entirely new, more productive user interface. Traditional dashboard interfaces present the business users with a multitude of seemingly unrelated charts and tables. The data discovery process of trying to find something of interest in the charts and tables (that is, slicing and dicing, drill across, drill down) is left to the user. However leveraging the insights-lead analytic process, the user interface can be simplified to present only the information or insights needed to run or optimize the business. Think how the iPod revolutionized the established MP3 market by providing a fundamentally simpler user interface—one that presented only those capabilities that enabled anyone to play the songs and the playlists that they wanted to play. With the advanced analytics enabled by big data, the user interface could focus on the delivery of two key pieces of information—insights and recommendations.

Insights are unusual behaviors or performance (for example, two standard deviations outside normal performance, 200 percent above or below predicted performance) that might require further investigation by the user. Insights would leverage both simple (time series trends, previous period comparisons, benchmarks) and advanced (predictive analytics, data mining, regression analysis) analytic models to identify performance situations operating outside of normal boundaries. These insights would be starting points for a more detailed investigation by the user. A few example insights are:

- Did you know that product A's sales to the [Soccer Dads] customer segment is 150 percent of what it was last period?
- Did you know that marketing campaign [2011 Back to School Sale] is 50 percent below forecasted conversions with only 2 weeks left in the campaign?
- Did you know that the variance level on machine [Charles City Plant Turbine 120] is 20 percent outside the normal control boundaries?

Recommendations are specific actions that are generated based on a detailed analysis of the insights and current state of the business. Recommendations would leverage advanced analytic modeling and real-time feeds to analyze the key business drivers and variables, update or fine-tune analytic models, and make specific recommendations. A few examples of recommendations are:

- We recommend marking down the product category [Christmas Lights] by 25 percent starting December 9, and increasing the markdown to 50 percent on December 16.

- We recommend increasing the media budget by 22 percent on display ad [Chevy Suburban] and decrease media budget 33 percent on display ad [Chevy Volt] for the remainder of the campaign [Holiday Season].
- We recommend repairing your [Maytag Model 3200] washer's drum engine within the next 5 days because there is a 95 percent probability of product failure.
- We recommend that patient A101-23V be admitted into the hospital for an extra day due to the high probability of readmission.

The user interface could start with these Insights and Recommendations, priority-ranked by their potential impact on the business. If the user then wanted more details on the Insights or Recommendations, they would select a More button to get the supporting details. If the user wanted to act on the given recommendation, they would select the Activate button (see Figure 5-3).

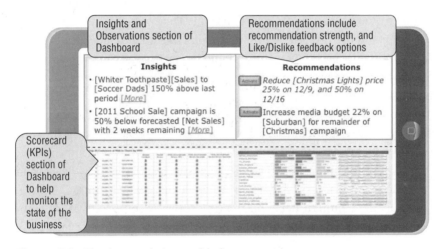

Figure 5-3: Big data analytics-enabled user experience

The analytics that underpin the insights and recommendations can be quite complex, but such analytic complexities are likely not of concern to the business user. The business user wants to have the data tell them what's happening in their business, and wants the technology to make recommendations based on previous learning and best practices. Also, the analytics can be personalized and self-learning so that it is constantly fine-tuning the analytic models based upon the user's feedback on what they like, don't like, and why (think about how Pandora, the online music service, uses "like" and "dislike" feedback to learn more about your music preferences).

Massive, detailed data sources, coupled with more powerful analytic tools, provides the capabilities to identify significant, material, and actionable insights in the data without forcing users to have the analytic skills or training to quantify why things happened. It enables a completely different user interface—one that is focused on providing greatly simplified insights and recommendations—to help business users optimize their key business processes.

The Human Challenge of Decision Making

Organizations are looking to use big data to become more analytics-driven in their business decision-making processes. However, there are several challenges that need to be addressed in order to make that transformation successful. One of those challenges is the very nature of how humans make decisions, and how our genetic makeup works against us in analyzing data and making decisions.

The human brain is a poor decision-making tool. Human decision making capabilities have evolved over millions of years of survival on the savanna. Humans have become very good at pattern recognition: from "That looks like just a harmless log behind that patch of grass," to "Yum, that looks like an antelope!" to "YIKES, that's a saber-toothed tiger!!" Necessity dictated that we become very good at recognizing patterns and making quick, instinctive survival decisions based on those patterns.

Unfortunately, humans are lousy number crunchers (guess we didn't need to crunch many numbers to spot that saber-toothed tiger). Consequently, humans have learned to rely on heuristics, gut feel, rules of thumb, anecdotal information, and intuition as decision guides. But these decision tricks are inherently flawed and fail us in a world of very large, widely varied, high velocity data sources.

Awareness of these human decision-making flaws is important if we want to transform our organization, and our people, into an analytics-driven business.

Traps in Decision Making

Let's cover a few examples of decision traps in which the human brain will lead to suboptimal, incorrect, or even fatal decisions.

Decision Trap #1: Overconfidence

We put a great deal of weight on whatever we happen to know, and assume that what we don't know isn't important. The casinos of Las Vegas were built on this human flaw (and why my son likes to say that "gambling is a tax on those who are bad at math").

For example, the hedge fund Long-Term Capital Management (LTCM), with two Nobel Prize winners on staff, returned approximately 40 percent per year from 1994 to 1998. Soon other traders started copying their techniques. So LTCM looked for new markets where others might not be able to mimic them. LTCM made the fatal assumption that these new markets operated in the same way as the old markets. In 1998, the LTCM portfolio dropped from $100 billion to $0.6 billion in value and a consortium of investment banks had to take LTCM over to avoid a market crash.

Companies make similar mistakes by overvaluing their experience in an existing market when they move into a new market (for example, AT&T with computers), or launch a new product into a different product category (such as Procter & Gamble with orange juice). Companies don't do enough research and analysis to identify and model the business drivers and the competitive and market risks of moving into a new market or product category. The following briefly summarizes this trap:

- **The Trap:** Humans put greater weight on whatever we happen to know and assume that what they don't know isn't important.
- **Business example:** Companies overvalue their experience from their existing market when they move into a new market and don't do enough research to understand the differences and risks of moving into that market.
- **Avoiding the Trap:**
    - Implement structured decision-making process
    - Do the research to gather all the facts and understand the risks
    - Use Review Boards

Decision Trap #2: Anchoring Bias

Anchoring is the subtle human tendency to latch onto one fact and use it as a reference point for decisions, even though that reference point may have no logical relevance to the decision at hand. During normal decision-making, individuals anchor, or overly rely, on specific information and then adjust to that value to account for other elements of the circumstance. Usually once the anchor is set, there is a bias toward that information.

For example, humans struggle deciding when to sell a stock. If someone buys a stock at $20 and then sees it rise to $80, they have a hard time selling the stock when it starts to drop because we've been anchored by the $80 price. This was a fairly common occurrence during the dot-com bust, as people saw their low-cost stock options rise to unimaginable highs, then rode their stock options (chased the tape) all the way to zero because they had set their anchor point too high.

This anchoring bias tends to show up in organizations' pricing, investment, and acquisition decisions. The following briefly summarizes this trap.

- **The Trap:** Subtle human tendency to glom onto one fact as a reference point for decisions, even though it may have no logical relevance to the decision at hand.

- **Business example:** You buy a stock at $20 and watch it rise to $80, but when the stock drops to $40 you refuse to sell and take the profits because you've been anchored by the $80 price.
- **Avoiding the Trap:**
  - Seek input from a variety of experts
  - Develop models to understand the business dynamics and relationships
  - Make planning a continuous process, not an event

Decision Trap #3: Risk Aversion

Our tolerance for risk is highly inconsistent. *Risk aversion* is a manifestation of people's general preference for certainty over uncertainty, and for minimizing the magnitude of the worst possible outcomes to which they are exposed. Risk aversion surfaces in the reluctance of a person to accept a bargain with an uncertain payoff rather than another bargain with a more certain, but possibly lower, expected payoff.

For example, a risk-averse investor might choose to put his or her money into a bank account with a low but guaranteed interest rate, rather than into a stock that may have high expected returns but also involves a chance of losing value. Another example is the reluctance of a business to cannibalize an incumbent product, even an aging or falling incumbent product, at the expense of an up-and-coming product. The following briefly summarizes this trap.

- **The Trap:** Human tolerance for risk is highly inconsistent.
- **Business example:** Companies invest in struggling traditional products at the expense of up-and-comers; companies are afraid to cannibalize their incumbent products, even when competitors are doing so.
- **Avoiding the Trap:**
  - Employ a structured process that captures and weighs both the risks as well as the opportunity costs of doing nothing
  - Use outside experts to minimize political anchors

Decision Trap #4: Don't Understand Sunk Costs

Many companies often throw good money after bad investments because they don't comprehend the concept of sunk costs. In economics, sunk costs are retrospective (past) costs that have already been incurred and cannot be recovered. Sunk costs are sometimes contrasted with prospective costs, which are future costs that may be incurred or changed if an action is taken. However, sunk costs need to be ignored when making going-forward decisions.

For example, people will sit through a bad movie until the end even though they are not enjoying the movie. Why? Most of us would watch the rest of the movie since we paid for it, but the truth is, the price of the movie is a sunk cost.

As business examples, Coca Cola (with New Coke) and IBM (with OS/2) continued to throw good money at bad investment decisions because they had invested significant time and money (and emotional capital) into those products and wanted to try to recoup their investments, even at the cost of missing more lucrative business opportunities. We see this today with on-going marketing campaign spend, brand rationalization decisions, and reluctance to exit poorly performing markets or product categories. The following briefly summarizes this trap.

- **The Trap:** People often throw good money after bad because they don't comprehend the concept of "sunk costs."
- **Business examples:** New Coke, IBM's OS/2, Microsoft Digital Marketing
- **Avoiding the Trap:**
    - Create business models that properly treat sunk costs as sunk costs
    - Ensure that analysis only considers new incremental costs
    - Use outside experts to minimize political anchors

Decision Trap #5: Framing

How a decision is stated or framed can impact what decision is made. Information, when presented in different formats, alters people's decisions. Individuals have a tendency to select inconsistent choices, depending on whether the question is framed to concentrate on losses or gains.

For example, participants were offered two alternative solutions for 600 people affected by a hypothetical deadly disease:

- Option A saves the lives of 200 people (33 percent saved, 66 percent die).
- Option B has a 33 percent chance of saving all 600 people and a 66 percent possibility of saving no one.

These decisions have the same expected value of 200 lives saved, but option B is risky. Of the two options, 72 percent of participants chose option A, whereas only 28 percent of participants chose option B.

However, another group of participants were offered the same scenario with the same statistics, but described differently:

- If option C is taken, 400 people will die.
- If option D is taken, there is a 33 percent chance that no people will die and a 66 percent probability that all 600 will die.

In this group, 78 percent of participants chose option D (equivalent to option B), whereas only 22 percent of participants chose option C (equivalent to option A).

The discrepancy in choice between these parallel options is the framing effect: the two groups favored different options because the options were expressed employing different language. In the first group, a positive frame emphasizes lives gained; in the second, a negative frame emphasizes lives lost. The following briefly summarizes this trap.

- **The Trap:** How a decision is stated or framed can impact what decision is made. Individuals have a tendency to select inconsistent choices, depending on whether the question is framed to concentrate on losses or gains.
- **Business examples:** Buying life insurance, 401-K enrollment
- **Avoiding the Trap:**
    - Ensure that the decision models use the same baseline and assumptions
    - Create models from multiple perspectives to ensure that the model weighs variables consistently

Other decision-making traps of which you need to be aware include:

- Herding (safety in numbers)
- Mental accounting
- Reluctance to admit mistakes (revisionist history)
- Confusing luck with skill
- Bias to the relative
- Overemphasizing the dramatic
- Regression to the mean
- Don't respect randomness

What Can One Do?

The key is to guide, not stifle, human intuition (think guardrails, not railroad tracks). Here are some things that you can do to guide your decision-making as you make the transformation to an analytics-driven organization:

- Use analytic models to help decision-makers understand and quantify the decision risks and returns. Leverage proven statistical tools and techniques to improve the understanding of probabilities. Employ a structured analytic discipline that captures and weighs both the risks and opportunities.
- Confirm and then reconfirm that you are using the appropriate metrics (think *Moneyball*). Just because a particular metric has always been the appropriate metric, don't assume that it is the right one for this particular decision.
- Challenge your model's assumptions. Test the vulnerability of the model and its assumptions using Sensitivity Analysis and Monte Carlo techniques.

For example, challenging the assumption that housing prices would never decline might have averted the recent mortgage market meltdown.

- Consult a wide variety of opinions when you vet a model. Avoid Group Think, which is yet another decision-making flaw. Group Think is a trap where you surround yourself with people who think like you. Consequently, the group is already predisposed to like and agree with whatever ideas and decisions you make. Have someone play the contrarian (think Tom Hanks in the movie *Big*). Use facilitation techniques in the decision process to ensure that all voices are heard and all views are contemplated.
- Be careful how you frame decisions.
- Create business models that properly treat sunk costs. Ensure that the model and analysis only consider new incremental costs. Ensure that your models include opportunity costs.
- Use "after the decision" review boards and formal debriefs to capture what worked, what didn't, and why.
- Beware of counterintuitive compensation; humans are revenue optimization machines.

Making the transformation to an analytics-driven culture is a powerful business enabler, but more than technology needs to be considered in driving that transformation. Understanding, managing, and educating people on common decision-making traps will help ensure a successful transformation.

Summary

This chapter covered how access to massive and diverse data sets is changing the way analysis is performed—organizations are spending less time understanding what caused something to happen and instead are acting more quickly on what the data is telling them to do. This approach does not work in all situations, as there are cases where it is important to understand why something happened (think medical care or triaging a major accident). But in many cases, the speed of making a decision is more important than getting the "perfect" decision (think use cases such as pricing, yield management, markdown management, ad serving, or fraud detection). To quote General George S. Patton, "A good plan violently executed now is better than a perfect plan executed next week."

Next you considered how the insights and recommendations that can be driven by big data and advanced analytics could impact the business user experience and the user interface. Instead of the traditional Business Intelligence model of giving users access to their data and hoping that they can slice and dice their way to insights (like trying to find the silver needle in a haystack of chrome needles), you can now leverage predictive analytics and real-time data feeds to uncover and publish insights and recommendations directly to the business users. That can dramatically impact the way the business users interact with data, and dramatically improve their productivity and business effectiveness.

Finally, you had a bit of fun considering how the human mind works against the best decision-making intentions. You considered human tendencies that short-circuit desired decision processes and lead to suboptimal, wrong or even fatal decisions. The chapter presented some techniques and processes that your organization can leverage to ensure that these traps in decision-making don't hinder your organization's ability to embrace data- or analytics-driven decision making.

6 Creating the Big Data Strategy

One of the key challenges IT organizations face in building support for a big data initiative is to ensure that the big data initiative is valued by, or of value to, the business stakeholders. Unfortunately, business stakeholders have become numb to the IT promises of the next great technology "silver bullet." They are hesitant to believe that another new technology is going to solve all of their data and analytic problems. Time and time again, the business stakeholders have been misled about the ease-of-use and the capabilities of these new technologies. This has led to walls being built between the IT and business teams.

You are now going to be introduced to a document that will ensure the business relevance of your big data initiative. While this exercise is not trivial, it does provide a repeatable process and framework to ensure that your big data efforts support the business's key initiatives. The document enforces a discipline that any organization can follow, as long as you truly understand and are focused on your organization's key business initiatives. The document is:

- Concise in that it fits onto a single page so that anyone can review it quickly to ensure they are working on the top priority items.
- Clear in defining what the organization and individuals need to do and accomplish in order to achieve the targeted strategic initiatives.
- Relevant to the business stakeholders by starting and focusing the process on supporting the organization's overall business strategy, and identifying the supporting business initiatives before diving into the technology, architecture, data, and analytic requirements.

The Big Data Strategy Document

The Big Data Strategy Document is comprised of the following sections, which are summarized in Figure 6-1:

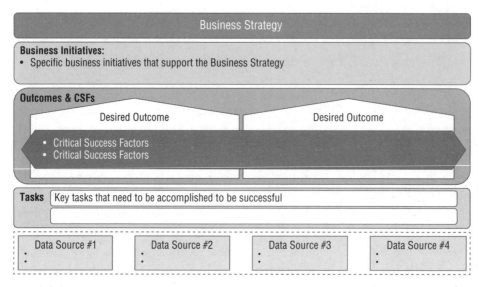

Figure 6-1: The Big Data Strategy Document

- **Business Strategy:** The targeted business strategy is captured as the title of the document and clearly defines the scope upon which the big data initiative will be focused. The title should not be more than one sentence, but should still provide enough detail to clearly identify the overall business objective, for example: "Improve customer intimacy" or "Reduce operational maintenance costs" or "Improve new product launch effectiveness."

- **Business Initiatives:** This section breaks down the business strategy into its supporting business initiatives. A business initiative is defined as a cross-functional project lasting 9 to 12 months in duration, with clearly stated financial or business goals against which success of the business initiative will be measured. Note that there should not be more than three to five business initiatives per business strategy. More than that and you have a wish list.

- **Outcomes and Critical Success Factors (CSF):** This section captures the outcomes and critical success factors necessary to support the successful execution of the organization's key business initiatives. Outcomes define the desired or ideal end state. Critical success factors define "what needs to be done" for the business initiative to be successful.

- **Tasks:** This section provides the next level of detail by documenting the specific tasks that need to be executed to perfection to be successful in support of the targeted business initiatives. These are the key tasks around which the different parts of the organization will need to collaborate to achieve the business initiatives. This is the "how to do it" section of the document, and it is at this level of detail where personal assignments and management objectives can be defined, assigned, and measured. One would normally expect 8 to 12 key tasks being identified and linked to the targeted business initiatives as part of the Big Data Strategy Document.
- **Data Sources:** Finally, the document highlights the key data sources required to support the business strategy and the supporting key business initiatives. From the definition of the tasks, you should have a strong understanding of the key metrics and measures, important business dimensions, level of granularity, and frequency of data access.

Customer Intimacy Example

To help make the Big Data Strategy Document come to life, let's walk through an example using a customer intimacy example (see Figure 6-2).

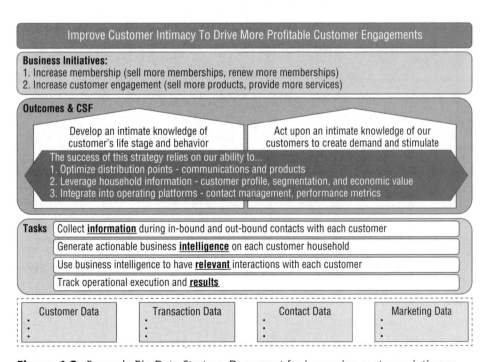

Figure 6-2: Example Big Data Strategy Document for improving customer intimacy

Business Strategy

The title of the document states the business strategy upon which the big data initiative is focused, in this case, "Improve customer intimacy to drive more profitable customer engagements." The title sets the scope of the strategy—you're focused on improving customer relationships, not improving predictive maintenance of network components—but you can see that this is not yet enough detail to be actionable.

Business Initiatives

This section captures the business initiatives that support the customer intimacy business strategy. These business initiatives capture the desired end goals, outline what the business hopes to achieve, and define how success will be measured. Examples of relevant business initiatives to support the customer intimacy business strategy could include:

- Increase memberships, such as sell more memberships, renew more memberships, or leverage advocacy to drive new memberships.
- Increase customer engagement, such as sell more products, provide more services, or co-market complementary services.

Outcomes and Critical Success Factors

This section contains the "what needs to be done" details to support the successful execution of the customer intimacy business initiatives. Examples of relevant CSFs could include:

- Develop an intimate understanding of your customer's life stage, behaviors, and areas of interests.
- Act upon an intimate knowledge of your customers to create demand and stimulate purchases.
- Optimize distribution or customer contact points through customer communications and customer-centric products and services.
- Acquire and leverage additional member and household information including customer profile, segmentation, and economic value.
- Integrate customer insights and actionable recommendations into operating platforms including contact management, performance metrics, and analysis tools.

Tasks

This section provides the next level of detail regarding the specific tasks around which the different organizations will need to collaborate to successfully execute against the different business initiatives (or the "how to do it" stage). This could include the following tasks (again, there are likely 8 to 12 of these tasks).

- Collect information (via increased use of surveys, question asking, and online instrumentation) during in-bound and out-bound contacts with each customer
- Generate actionable intelligence on each customer household
- Use that actionable intelligence to have relevant interactions with each customer
- Track operational execution and results

Data Sources

Finally, the document highlights some of the key data sources required to support the key business initiatives. In this case, you would need the following data sources to start:

- Customer data (demographic, behavioral, psycho-demographic)
- Transaction data (purchases, returns)
- Contact data (consumer comments, e-mail threads, social media dialogues)
- Marketing data (campaign spend, leads, conversions)

Turning the Strategy Document into Action

Now that you have the Big Data Strategy Document with the stated business strategy, business initiatives, critical success factors, key tasks, and data sources defined, the next stage is to identify the supporting business intelligence (BI), advanced analytics, and data warehouse requirements (see Figure 6-3).

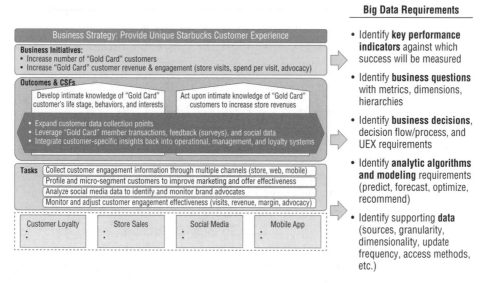

Figure 6-3: Big Data Strategy Document identifies supporting big data requirements

The strategy document breaks the technology requirements into the following components:

- Identify the metrics, measures, and key performance indicators against which the progress and success of each of the business initiatives will be measured.
- Identify the business questions, metrics, and dimensions (using "by" analysis) necessary to support the business initiatives. You should also capture any hierarchical business relationships at this stage.
- Identify the business decisions and the flow of the decisions required to support each key task. Test or prototype these key tasks and decisions to validate that you have captured all the necessary business questions, metrics/facts, and dimensions. Capture the business decisions, decision flow/process, and user experience (UEX) requirements
- Identify the analytic algorithms and data modeling and transformations required to support the predictive components of each of the key tasks. Look for opportunities to insert new predictive "verbs," such as score, forecast, optimize, recommend, and predict, into the business questions and business decisions.
- Identify the supporting data sources including measures, dimensionality, dimensional attributes, granularity, update frequency, storage location, and access methods.

As a result of this work, you are now in a position to define the technology stack and required data and analytics architecture including the Master Data Management (MDM), ETL/ELT/data enrichment, data warehousing, BI, and advanced analytics requirements necessary to support the Customer Intimacy business strategy.

Starbucks Big Data Strategy Document Example

Let's walk through another example of the Big Data Strategy Document using Starbucks, a company of which I am a big fan and one of their many Gold Card members. Below is an excerpt from the Starbucks 2011 Annual Report that will help guide development of the Big Data Strategy Document for Starbucks (see quote below). (It should be noted that all of the data used in this Starbucks example is available from public sources, and the development of the Starbucks Big Data Strategy Document is based entirely on my personal experience consuming Starbucks products and using their website, mobile app and stores.)

Our retail objective is to be the leading retailer and brand of coffee *in each of our target markets by selling the finest quality coffee and related products, by* **providing each customer a unique Starbucks Experience**. *The Starbucks Experience is built upon superior customer service as well as clean and well-maintained company-operated stores that reflect the personalities of the communities in which they operate, thereby building a high degree of customer loyalty.*

—Starbucks 2011 Annual Report

From the 2011 Starbucks annual report, you can see that Starbucks has a business strategy focused on "…providing each customer a unique Starbucks Experience." Building upon that stated business strategy, you would use the process articulated earlier in this chapter to build a Starbucks' Big Data Strategy Document and break down their strategy into its business, and eventually big data, requirements (see Figure 6-4).

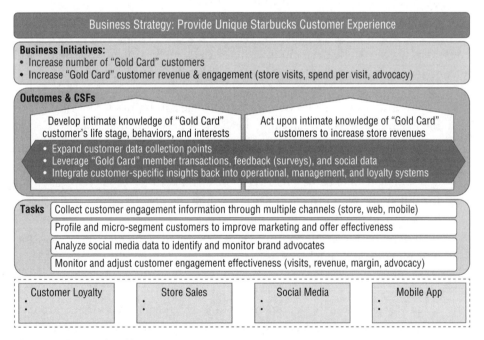

Figure 6-4: Starbuck's Big Data Strategy Document

First, you want to identify the two to four key business initiatives that support the "Provide a Unique Starbucks Customer Experience" business strategy. A couple of supporting key business initiatives could be:

■ Increase number of Gold Card customers from six million to nine million over the next 12 months.

■ Increase Gold Card customer revenue and customer engagement by increasing store visits, spend per visit, advocacy, and likelihood to recommend for each Gold Card member. (Ideally there would be a target number for each of these key customer engagement metrics.)

There are likely a few more business initiatives that Starbucks would declare to support their "Provide a Unique Starbucks Customer Experience" business strategy, but let's focus on just these two for now.

Next you want to identify the desired outcomes that Starbucks would want to achieve to support these business initiatives. These desired outcomes could include:

■ Develop intimate knowledge of Gold Card customers' life stage, personal behaviors and preferences, and areas of interests and passion.

■ Act upon the Gold Card customers' intimate knowledge to increase store revenues while improving the overall Starbucks customer "experience."

You also need to define the supporting critical success factors, which could include:

■ Expand the number of customer data collection points leveraging social media, the Starbucks mobile app, the website, and more traditional customer communication techniques such as direct mail, e-mail, and surveys.

■ Leverage "Gold Card" member transactions, feedback (surveys), and social and mobile data to paint a more complete and accurate picture (persona) of the different Gold Card customer types or segments.

■ Uncover and then integrate customer-specific insights back into operational (call centers, direct marketing, store ops), management (store reporting and management dashboards), and loyalty systems (customer service, marketing).

Next, the Big Data Strategy Document captures the specific tasks that Starbucks needs its different business functions to execute. This is where the rubber meets the road, and how the "Provide a Unique Starbucks Customer Experience" business strategy translates into the day-to-day operations of each Starbucks employee. These key tasks could include:

■ Provide additional and improved opportunities to collect customer engagement information through multiple channels including in-store, web, social media, and mobile devices.

- Profile and micro-segment customers to improve marketing and offering effectiveness; focus on doubling the number of profiled customer segments by end of year.
- Analyze social media data to identify and monitor brand advocates; measure and monitor Gold Card customers' Likelihood to Recommend (LTR).
- Monitor, measure, and adjust customer engagement effectiveness including number of visits, revenue per visit, margin per visit, market basket propensities, and brand advocacy.

Finally, you determine the data sources necessary to support Starbucks' business strategy and key business initiatives. These data sources could include:

- Customer demographic, lifestyle, location preferences, and associated behavioral data
- Customer product purchase history
- Store product sales data
- Social media postings and sentiment
- Mobile app location data (coupled with product purchase data)

What's useful about this Big Data Strategy Document development process is that it not only defines the data sources and analytic capabilities upon which the organization needs to focus to successfully support the business strategy, but it also defines what data sources and analytic capabilities are *not* needed at this point in time. It provides the guardrails that help the organization stay focused while simultaneously developing the longer-term big data capabilities and providing a business relevant roadmap for introducing new big data technologies and innovations.

You are now in a position to identify the data management, data platform, business intelligence, and analytic requirements to support Starbucks' "Provide a Unique Starbucks Customer Experience" business strategy.

San Francisco Giants Big Data Strategy Document Example

Let's demonstrate the versatility of the Big Data Strategy Document to accomplish something that may seem a bit more whimsical: winning the World Series. Let's say that you are the general manager of a professional baseball team. You have been chartered by ownership to "Win the World Series." (I am convinced that there are teams where "Win the World Series" is not their goal, but instead have a goal to just make profits without regard to the quality of play on the field, but that's the cynical Chicago Cubs fan in me coming out.)

Like in any commercial business, there are multiple business strategies that a baseball organization could pursue to achieve the "Win the World Series" goal, including:

- Spend huge amounts of money for veteran, proven, top-performing players (New York Yankees, Boston Red Sox, and Los Angeles Dodgers)
- Spend huge amounts of money for over-the-hill, inconsistent performing players (the Chicago Cubs seem to have mastered this strategy, though the New York Mets seem to be trying to perfect this approach as well)
- Spend top money to have outstanding starting and relief pitching, and scrounge together enough timely hitting to win games (San Francisco Giants)
- Spend top money to have outstanding hitting and hope that you can piece together enough pitching to win games (Texas Rangers, Los Angeles Angels)
- Spend miserly amounts of money and rely upon your minor league systems to bring up quality, low paid, rookie players (Oakland A's, Minnesota Twins, and Tampa Bay Rays)

So using the Big Data Strategy Document, let's play General Manager of the San Francisco Giants to see what they would need to do to be successful in their goal of winning the World Series.

The first step is to clearly articulate your business strategy. In the case of the San Francisco Giants, I'd say that their business strategy for winning the World Series would be to "Acquire and retain high-performing, sustainable starting and relief pitching to compete annually for the World Series."

Remember that a business strategy is typically three or more years in scope. If you change your business strategy annually, then that's not a strategy (sounds more like a fad). But companies do and should change their business strategies based upon changing economic conditions, market forces, customer demographic trends, technology changes, and even new insights from big data analytics (which might reveal that strong pitching tends—from a statistical perspective—to beat strong hitting in the post season). This seems to be what the San Francisco Giants did when they moved away from a "long ball" business strategy in trying to reach the World Series (by surrounding Barry Bonds with other strong batters) to their current "superior starting pitching" business strategy.

So let's use the Big Data Strategy Document to see what you (the Giants General Manager) need to do to successfully execute the "superior starting and relief pitching to win the World Series" business strategy.

First, you want to identify the two to four key business initiatives that support the "superior starting and relief pitching to win the World Series" business strategy.

Business initiatives are cross-functional plans, typically 9 to 12 months in length, with clearly defined financial or business metrics. For this baseball exercise, I'm only going to list two (although I can think of two more that also need to be addressed in the case of the San Francisco Giants):

- Acquire and maintain throughout the season top-tier starting pitchers as measured by quality starts (pitches at least six innings in a start), Earned Run Average (ERA), Walks and Hits per Inning Pitched (WHIP), strikeout-to-walk ratio, and number of home runs allowed per nine innings.
- Perfect "small ball" offensive strategy as measured by On Base Percentage (OBP), batting average with runners in scoring position, stealing percentage, hit-and-run execution, and sacrifice hitting effectiveness.

Next, you want to identify the desired outcomes from your business initiatives, which in this case could include:

- Develop detailed knowledge and predictive insights into individual pitcher in-game and situational pitching tendencies (by competitors, specific batters, ballpark, weather conditions, days of rest, etc.).
- Develop detailed knowledge and predictive insights into hitter tendencies and behaviors with runners in scoring positions (by count, number of outs, competitive pitcher, who's on base, or day versus night).

Next, you want to identify the critical success factors necessary to support the business initiatives, including:

- Expand pitching and hitting performance observations and predictive insights accuracy; that is, experiment with other data sources to create composite measures that might be better predictors of pitching and hitting performance.
- Predict player development of starting pitching candidates (whether in your minor league system or not, including existing relief pitchers and potential draft and free agent candidates).
- Integrate pitching and hitting insights and probabilities into the managerial and in-game decision support systems given player current performance trends and behaviors by opponent, opponent's pitcher, game situation, time of day, time of year, weather conditions, etc.

Next, identify the key tasks that you must execute successfully (perfectly?) in order to achieve your desired state, including:

■ Collect and monitor starting pitching performance and behavioral data in order to preserve end-of-season pitching capabilities (in other words, you don't want to wear out your starting pitching).

■ Analyze current pitching performance trends to optimize starter and in-game relief pitching decisions (develop the statistics and metrics to better predict when to pull a starting pitcher and what relievers to use in what game situations).

■ Optimize the portfolio of "small ball" hitting capabilities through minor league personnel, development, promotions, and trades (constantly be looking for hitters that can fill holes or improve on your current "small ball" hitting portfolio).

■ Deploy player-specific hitting insights for in-game decisions in order to optimize steal, hit-and-run, and sacrifice opportunities.

Finally, identify the data that you will need to support the entire process, including:

■ Detailed personnel information including key personal health history (weight, health, injuries, medication), performance history (60-yard dash time, long toss distances, fastball velocity), and workout history (bench press, dead lift, crunches in 60 seconds, number of workouts).

■ Pitcher Game Statistics History including number of pitches thrown, strike-to-ball ratio, strikeouts-to-walk ratio, WHIP, ERA, first-pitch strikes, batting average against, and slugging percentage against per year and per game.

■ Hitting Game Statistics History including OBP, slugging percentage, and hitting with runners on base per year and per game.

■ Competitive Information including batting averages, walks, strikeouts, home runs per nine innings, and slugging percentages for each competitive batter (against right or left handers, by ballparks, by time of day, by time of year).

■ Stadium Information including length down the lines, length to deep center, average temperatures by day of year, average humidity by day of year (very important for knuckleballers), altitude, etc.

There are other data sources to contemplate, including weather conditions at game time, performance numbers of the game's top historical pitchers (for benchmarking purposes), performance numbers for current pitchers (again, for benchmarking purposes), and economic costs (salary, bonuses, etc.).

Figure 6-5 shows the resulting Big Data Strategy Document.

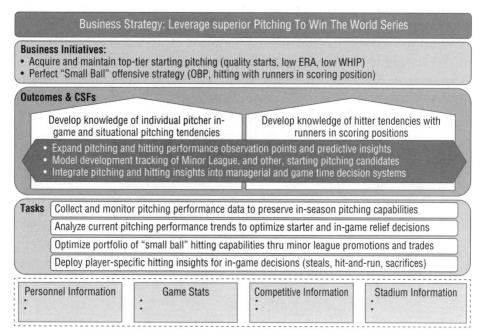

Business Strategy: Leverage superior Pitching To Win The World Series

Business Initiatives:
- Acquire and maintain top-tier starting pitching (quality starts, low ERA, low WHIP)
- Perfect "Small Ball" offensive strategy (OBP, hitting with runners in scoring position)

Outcomes & CSFs

| Develop knowledge of individual pitcher in-game and situational pitching tendencies | Develop knowledge of hitter tendencies with runners in scoring positions |

- Expand pitching and hitting performance observation points and predictive insights
- Model development tracking of Minor League, and other, starting pitching candidates
- Integrate pitching and hitting insights into managerial and game time decision systems

Tasks
- Collect and monitor pitching performance data to preserve in-season pitching capabilities
- Analyze current pitching performance trends to optimize starter and in-game relief decisions
- Optimize portfolio of "small ball" hitting capabilities thru minor league promotions and trades
- Deploy player-specific hitting insights for in-game decisions (steals, hit-and-run, sacrifices)

| Personnel Information | Game Stats | Competitive Information | Stadium Information |

Figure 6-5: The San Francisco Giants' Big Data Strategy Document for winning the World Series

So playing the San Francisco Giants' general manager was a fun exercise that provides another perspective on how to use the Big Data Strategy Document, not only to break down your organization's business strategy and key business initiatives into the required critical success factors and key tasks, but ultimately to lead to the appropriate data strategy and big data analytics architecture requirements.

Summary

This chapter covers several topics. It goes into detail on the use of the Big Data Strategy Document to ensure alignment between your big data initiatives and what the business thinks is materially important—the overall business strategy. The Big Data Strategy Document drives alignment between the business stakeholders and IT, while also acting as a guide against which data and technology decisions can be made. The strategy document helps prioritize the technology requirements by gauging them against their ability to support the targeted business strategy, key business initiatives, critical success factors, and key tasks.

Two examples of Big Data Strategy Document development were used—Starbucks and the San Francisco Giants—to help you understand how to build your own Big Data Strategy Document. It is not a hard process, but it does require the cooperation of key business stakeholders and their supporting IT organization in order to complete the document, which likely is the first test for how serious an organization is in leveraging big data to materially transform their business operations and rewire their value creation processes.

7 Understanding Your Value Creation Process

Some organizations have a hard time understanding or "envisioning" how big data can power their key business initiatives. This is especially true of the business users who do not understand the types of questions that can be answered and the decisions they can make by leveraging big data. This chapter introduces several envisioning techniques and exercises—with supporting worksheets—that can help business users, as well as IT teams, understand where and how big data can impact the key business value creation processes.

The envisioning exercises facilitate brainstorming among the business users to identify specific areas where big data can impact their business. These envisioning exercises are especially effective when conducted as part of a larger ideation workshop environment where group dynamics and the sharing of ideas can fuel the idea creation process.

Two basic premises underpin the use of these envisioning exercises:

1. The business users know what types of questions they are trying to answer in support of their key business processes.
2. The business users understand what types of decisions they are trying to make today in support of their key business processes.

As discussed in Chapter 3, I think you will find that the types of questions users are trying to answer are likely the same questions that organizations have been trying to answer for several decades. These are questions such as: Who are my most valuable customers? What are my most important products? What are my most successful campaigns? (See Figure 7-1.)

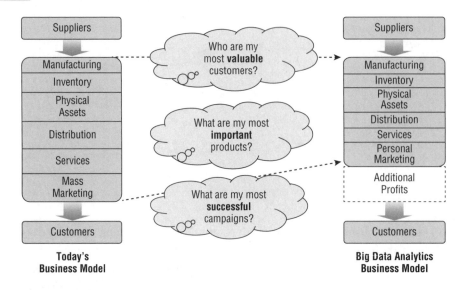

Figure 7-1: Big data drives value creation processes.

Business users need to answer these types of questions in order to:

- Uncover new revenue opportunities that impact their marketing and sales organizations
- Reduce costs in their procurement, manufacturing, inventory, supply chain, distribution, marketing, sales and service, and support functions
- Mitigate risks across all operational and financial aspects of the organization's value chain
- Garner new customer, product, and operational insights that they can use to gain competitive advantage over their competitors and extract more profit from the industry

What has changed with big data is how you can leverage new sources of data and new analytic capabilities to answer these key business questions to uncover new insights about your customers, products, and markets. For example, the question about our "most important customers" previously was determined by identifying the customers who bought the most products (take your product sales data, sort in descending order, and the customers at the top are your most important). Then the "most important customers" question was answered with our most *profitable* customers (integrate sales, returns, payments, product margin, call center, and commissions data to calculate your most profitable customers). Nowadays, the "most important customers" question is answered with our most *influential* customers (take data from a multitude of social media sites to determine the range of influence and level of advocacy for each customer, and aggregate the profitability of each of their friends to calculate the "range of influence" profitability). As you can see, as new data has been made available, the level granularity at which you can answer the most important, valuable, and successful types of questions has been taken to the next level of fidelity, but has also increased the complexity of those answers almost exponentially.

Big data enables you to answer those questions and make those decisions at the next level of detail in order to uncover new insights about your customers, products, and operations, and apply those new insights to answer those key business questions such as the most valuable, most important, and most successful at a higher-fidelity and in a timelier manner. Big data fine-tunes and accelerates your ability to identify the specific areas of the business and specific business processes where big data can deliver immediate business value.

Understanding the Big Data Value Creation Drivers

Think of this chapter as an introductory course in the Big Data MBA (Masters of Business Administration). I'm going to introduce many MBA concepts as a way to help organizations envision where and how big data could impact their value creation processes.

The key to the big data envisioning and value creation process is to understand the "big data business drivers." There are four big data business drivers (see Table 7-1) that can be applied to an organization's key business initiatives or business processes to provide new insights about the business (across customers, products, operations, markets, etc.) and improve decision-making. Let's walk through each of the four big data business drivers.

Table 7-1: The Four Big Data Business Drivers

Big Data Business Drivers	Data Monetization Impacts
Structured Data: More detailed transactional data (e.g., POS, CDR, RFID, Credit card)	Enable more granular, more detailed decisions (local, seasonal, multi-dimensional)
Unstructured Data: Diverse internal (e-mail, consumer comments) and external (social media, mobile) unstructured data	Enable more complete, more accurate decisions unstructured (with new metrics, dimensions, and dimensional attributes)
Data Velocity: Low-latency ("real-time") data access	Enable more frequent, more timely decisions (hourly vs. weekly, on-demand)
Predictive Analytics: Causality, predictors, instrumentation, experimentation	More actionable, predictive decisions (optimize, recommend, predict, score, forecast)

Driver #1: Access to More Detailed Transactional Data

Access to more detailed, more granular, structured (transactional) data enables a higher degree of fidelity to the questions that the business users are trying to answer and decisions that the business users are trying to make. For example, what types of questions could I answer and what decisions could I make if I had the ability to access and analyze more detailed transactional data, such as point-of-sale (POS) transactions, call detail records, radio frequency identification (RFID), credit card transactions, stock transactions, insurance claims, and medical health readings?

Access to more detailed transactional data is probably the "lowest hanging fruit" for most organizations—to take advantage of the transactional data, sometimes called "dark" data, they already collect. Due to today's technology limitations and data warehouse cost factors, most business users only have access to a limited amount of data that is supporting their operational and management reporting. However, big data technologies provide the ability to access and analyze all the detailed and granular transactional data. Access to all the detailed transactional data can fuel the creative juices of the business user to ask more insightful "what if" questions, such as:

- What's the potential business value of supporting more localization by developing forecasts and product plans at the product category, store, and department levels?
- What's the potential business value of supporting more seasonal decision-making by developing marketing plans at the customer segment, product, ZIP code, and season levels (such as Christmas, 4th of July, Valentine's Day)?
- What's the potential business value of triaging claims patterns at the policy type by rider, claim, week, or day levels?
- What's the potential business value of making network capacity and utilization forecasts based at the ZIP+4, local events, and season levels?

As you can see, the potential to analyze your existing transactional data across multiple dimensions of the business—dimensions like location (specific outlets, branches, or stores), product, day of week, time of day, holiday, customer behavioral category, customer demographic category, and others—and at a lower level of granularity can dramatically improve your organization's ability to uncover actionable and material business opportunities.

Driver #2: Access to Unstructured Data

The ability to integrate the growing volumes of unstructured data with your existing detailed structured transactional data has the potential to radically transform the types of insights that can be teased out of the data. The unstructured data can provide new metrics and dimensions that can be used by the business stakeholders to uncover new insights about your customers, products, operations, and markets. For example, what is the potential business impact of having access to internal unstructured data (such as consumer comments, e-mails, physician notes, claims explanations) as well as external unstructured data (such as, social media, mobile, machine, or sensor generated)? The business users could leverage the new metrics, dimensions, and dimensional attributes gleaned from unstructured data sources, coupled with the detailed transactional data, for finer-fidelity, more complete analysis and decisions to answer questions such as:

- What's the business potential of leveraging new insights about my customers' interests, passions, associations, and affiliations (gleaned from social media activities) into my customer acquisition, maturation, and retention business processes?
- What's the business potential of adding sensor-generated performance data into your manufacturing, supply chain, and product predictive maintenance models?
- What's the business potential of integrating third-party unstructured data sources (local weather, economic news, local events) into hospital or doctor office staffing and patient care decisions?
- What's the business potential of integrating social media data into your claims fraud analysis to identify unusual claim submissions among communities of linked individuals?

Driver #3: Access to Low-latency (Real-time) Data

The ability to provide real-time (or low-latency) access to data is a game changer that can enable new monetization opportunities. The biggest problem with today's batch-centric data platforms is that many customer and market opportunities are fleeting—they appear and disappear before one has a chance to identify *and* act on them. Think, for example, of the business potential of location-based services to communicate to your customers in real-time as they are making their buying decisions. In other words, what is the business potential of having real-time or low-latency access to key data sources and business metrics in order to shrink the time between when a customer, product, or operational event occurs and when that data is available for analysis and decision-making? What is the business potential of being able to update your customer, product, risk, and operational analytic models on-demand, based on immediate business, market other external events events (such as your favorite baseball team winning the World Series, financial markets jumping 4 percent in a single day, or a destructive hurricane predicted within the next two days)?

Access to low-latency, real-time data can fuel the creative thought processes in the timeliness of the types of questions you could answer and decisions you could make, such as:

■ What's the business potential of making customer acquisition, predictive maintenance, or network optimization decisions on a minute, hourly, or "on-demand" basis?

■ What's the business potential of updating analytic models on-demand based on current market, economic, or local events (e.g., weather, traffic, concerts, professional football game)?

■ What's the business potential of continuously updating fraud detection models based upon unusual activities amongst a social group of users?

■ What's the business potential of updating hospital staffing and inventory requirements based on local health incidents or disease outbreaks?

■ What's the business potential of updating your distribution schedules and planned deliveries based on current weather, traffic conditions, and local entertainment or sporting events?

Driver #4: Integration of Predictive Analytics

The integration of predictive or advanced analytics into key business processes holds the potential to transform every question that business users are trying to answer, and every decision they are trying to make. This is really about introducing a whole new set of verbs to the business stakeholders—verbs such as predict, forecast, score, recommend, and optimize. These new verbs can help business users envision a whole new set of questions to ask around the potential business impact of predicting what could happen, recommending a specific course of action, or forecasting the impact of different decision scenarios.

Integrating predictive analytics into key business processes and getting business users to embrace these new verbs can produce more predictive answers to key questions, such as:

■ What's the business potential of leveraging predictive analytics to *optimize* network operations, marketing spending, and staffing decisions?

■ What's the business potential of leveraging predictive analytics to *predict* the financial impact of pricing, route, or supplier changes?

■ What's the business potential of leveraging predictive analytics to *score* customers for fraud, retention, up-sell, and likelihood to recommend (LTR)?

- What's the impact of *scoring* patients for treatment response and readmission likelihood?
- What's the business potential to *score* partners for quality, delivery, and service reliability?
- What's the business potential of leveraging predictive analytics to *forecast* network loads (based on economic conditions and local events) or forecast the performance of new product introductions (based on consumer sentiment and product category dynamics)?
- What's the business potential of leveraging predictive analytics to *recommend* next best offers to improve customer satisfaction, customer retention, or preventive patient treatment?

Big Data Envisioning Worksheet

The Big Data Envisioning Worksheet, shown in Table 7-2, is a tool for applying the four big data business drivers against your organization's targeted business initiative or business process. The worksheet, when used as part of an ideation workshop, facilitates the business users' creative thinking to envision the types of questions they could ask applying the big data business drivers. A sample worksheet is available for download at www.wiley.com/go/bigdataforbusiness.

Table 7-2: Big Data Envisioning Worksheet

Big Data Business Drivers	Targeted Business Initiative
Driver #1: What is the impact of more detailed, structured transactional data?	Detailed Transactional Data Brainstorm #1
	Detailed Transactional Data Brainstorm #2
	Detailed Transactional Data Brainstorm #3
Driver #2: What is the impact of internal and external unstructured data?	Unstructured Data Brainstorm #1
	Unstructured Data Brainstorm #2
	Unstructured Data Brainstorm #3
Driver #3: What is the impact of real-time, low-latency data access?	Real-time Data Access Brainstorm #1
	Real-time Data Access Brainstorm #2
	Real-time Data Access Brainstorm #3
Driver #4: What is the impact of predictive analytics?	Predictive Analytics Brainstorm #1
	Predictive Analytics Brainstorm #2
	Predictive Analytics Brainstorm #3

Let's walk through a few examples using the Big Data Envisioning Worksheet to see how to apply the four big data business drivers in some real-world situations.

Big Data Business Drivers: Predictive Maintenance Example

The first example comes from the railroad industry. A railroad company is trying to predict engine and railcar maintenance in order to be compliant with the Positive Train Control (PTC) mandate. The PTC goals are to eliminate runaway trains and train crashes. The same information can be used by train operators for predictive maintenance in order to optimize the scheduling of railcar and engine maintenance. The targeted business initiative would then be:

> *Predictive Maintenance: Predict engine and railcar maintenance to reduce runaway trains and train crashes, and to improve scheduling of railcar and engine maintenance.*

Driver #1

What is the potential impact on the targeted business initiative from having access to more detailed and granular transactional data? This could include the following:

- Leveraging railcar details (age, manufacturer, condition, location), usage history (length of runs, types of loads, utilization), and maintenance records (last service date, type of service, history of service) to create a railcar maintenance score (likelihood of railcar requiring maintenance)
- Trending and monitoring individual railcar and overall railcar maintenance activities across multiple dimensions including area of service, age of rail car, railcar manufacturer, type of load, length of service, and maintenance crew
- Identifying appropriate maintenance key performance indicators (KPIs) against which you can monitor and predict railcar performance and reliability

Driver #2

What is the potential impact on the targeted business initiative from having access to new sources of internal and external unstructured data? This could include:

- Integrating sensor data from key railcar components (ball bearings, couplers, axles, wheels, carriages) to improve railcar maintenance predictability
- Leveraging external weather (moisture, temperatures, ice) and seasonal (leaves on the tracks, snow levels) data to predict product performance stress situations
- Leveraging maintenance crew comments to identify railcar performance insights or railcar maintenance problems

Driver #3

What is the potential impact on the targeted business initiative from having real-time, low-latency data access? This could include the following:

- Supporting on-demand railcar maintenance scoring with real-time sensor data feeds integrated with local weather data
- Leveraging railcar scores, component inventory availability, maintenance crew skills, location, and schedules to optimize scheduling of railcar maintenance and minimize service parts inventory carrying costs

Driver #4

What is the potential impact of predictive analytics—predict, forecast, score, recommend, optimize—on the targeted business initiative? This could include:

- Using predictive analytics to optimize the scheduling of crew maintenance combined with inventory availability, inventory location, and weather/temperature forecasts to reduce the time railcars are offline for maintenance
- Using attribution analysis modeling to predict maintenance effectiveness across multiple dimensions including maintenance crew, history of maintenance, railcar manufacturer, area of service, types of loads, and others

Big Data Business Drivers: Customer Satisfaction Example

The next example is relevant for most companies, whether the company is in the Business-to-consumer (B2C) or Business-to-business (B2B) industries. In this example, you'll examine how an automotive manufacturer could leverage new sources of customer and product insights to predict the impact of their dealer service quality on customer satisfaction. The targeted business initiative would then be:

> *Customer Satisfaction Optimization: Monitor, score, and reward outstanding dealers to enhance customer loyalty and predict warranty liabilities and costs.*

Driver #1

What is the potential impact on the targeted business initiative from having access to more detailed and granular transactional data? This could include:

- Leveraging detailed parts orders, inventory, and returns data to identify product quality trends and flag potential parts shortages across dealers, markets, parts, and vehicles that could impact customer satisfaction with scheduling car maintenance
- Identifying appropriate customer satisfaction KPIs captured through post-service surveys against which to monitor dealer performance and flag product performance problems and trends

Driver #2

What is the potential impact on the targeted business initiative from having access to new sources of internal and external unstructured data? This could include the following:

- Integrating consumer comments from internal customer engagement sources—such as call centers, consumer comments, and e-mails—to identify reoccurring product and service quality problems
- Leveraging social media data, data gathered from specific websites, mobile apps (Kelly Blue Book, Yelp, Edmunds), and blog comments to benchmark the company's product and service quality against industry and specific competitors' performance
- Leveraging dealer service bay notes, dealer social media feeds, and manufacturer social media feeds to identify recurring parts and vehicle performance problems and negative service and product performance trends

Driver #3

What is the potential impact on the targeted business initiative from having real-time, low-latency data access? This could include:

- Monitoring social media sites daily for positive and negative sentiment spikes between own, competitive, and industry by product categories and location (city, ZIP code)
- Monitoring social media sites for changes in own versus competitive dealer service performance

Driver #4

What is the potential impact of predictive analytics—predict, forecast, score, recommend, optimize—on the targeted business initiative? This could include the following:

- Integrating social media data with internal consumer comments to score the company's dealer customer satisfaction (by vehicle, model, dealer, and location) and track changes in dealer satisfaction scores

- Analyzing social media data to monitor competitive dealer satisfaction and sentiment issues in order to recommend competitive "win back" marketing campaigns
- *Correlating* changes in social media service quality sentiment with personnel schedules in order to predict the impact that certain service personnel have on overall customer satisfaction

Big Data Business Drivers: Customer Micro-segmentation Example

The final example is relevant for B2C companies that are interested in increasing the effectiveness of their customer engagement and marketing initiatives. For example, organizations can move from just a few customer segments to thousands of customer micro-segments by leveraging the customer and product insights that are buried inside the multitude of unstructured customer interactions. From sources such as consumer comments, call center notes, e-mail threads, and social media postings, organizations can gain powerful insights into customers' interests, passions, associations, and affiliations that can dramatically improve the relevance and performance of each of the customer micro-segments. This will enable more targeted customer interactions via more focused marketing campaigns campaigns against these more granular customer segments.

For this example, the targeted business initiative would then be:

> *Customer Micro-segmentation: Increase the number of customer segments in order to improve customer profiling, segmentation, targeting, acquisition, maturation (cross-sell and up-sell), retention, and advocacy processes.*

Driver #1

What is the potential impact on the targeted business initiative from having access to more detailed and granular transactional data? This could include the following:

- Integrating detailed POS transactions with market basket, customer demographic, and behavioral data to create customer micro-segments based on demographics (age, gender), behavioral categories, geography, product categories, and seasonality

- Augmenting customer micro-segments with third-party customer data (from the Acxioms and Experians of the world, plus digital management platform data from providers such as BlueKai and nPario) to include income levels, wealth levels, education levels, household size, psycho-demographic data and online behaviors

Driver #2

What is the potential impact on the targeted business initiative from having access to new sources of internal and external unstructured data? This could include:

- Mining social media data to create richer micro-segmentation models based on customers' social insights including interests, passions, associations, and affiliations
- Leveraging mobile data (from smartphone apps) to create geography- or store-specific micro-segments

Driver #3

What is the potential impact on the targeted business initiative from having real-time, low-latency data access? This could include the following:

- Recalculating customer micro-segmentation models immediately after "significant" events such as the Oscars, the Olympics, or severe storms
- Updating customer acquisition up-sell and cross-sell (next best offer) scores and propensities daily while customer marketing campaigns are still active

Driver #4

What is the potential impact of predictive analytics—predict, forecast, score, recommend, and optimize—on the targeted business initiative? This could include:

- Using predictive analytics to score and predict the performance of the highest-potential customer micro-segments integrating POS transactions, market basket, customer loyalty, social media, and mobile data
- Using cross-media attribution modeling to optimize media spending across the highest potential customer segments
- Recommending best micro-segments to target given a particular campaign's audience, product awareness, and sales goals

The Big Data Envisioning Worksheet is a useful tool for helping business users envision where and how big data can power their key business initiatives. It applies the four big data drivers to uncover new business insights that can yield timelier, more complete, more accurate, and more frequent business decisions.

Michael Porter's Valuation Creation Models

Another envisioning technique involves the use of Michael Porter's popular and well-documented value creation models:

- Five Forces Analysis
- Value Chain Analysis

Porter's value creation models, much like the Big Data Envisioning Worksheet, provide another business valuation technique that you can use to identify where and how big data can impact your organization's value creation processes.

Michael Porter's Five Forces Analysis

Taken from Wikipedia's definition of Michael Porter's Five Forces Analysis:

> Porter's five forces analysis is a framework for industry analysis and business strategy development formed by Michael E. Porter of Harvard Business School in 1979. It draws on industrial organization economics to derive five forces that determine the competitive intensity and therefore attractiveness of a market. Attractiveness in this context refers to the overall industry profitability. An "unattractive" industry is one in which the combination of these five forces acts to drive down overall profitability. A very unattractive industry would be one approaching "pure competition," in which available profits for all firms are driven to normal profit.

The Five Forces Analysis provides an industry-wide, or outside-in, perspective on an organization's competitive drivers. These "Five Forces" or competitive drivers are the following:

1. *Competitive Rivalry* factors include the number and size of firms competing in the industry, overall industry size, key industry trends and directions, break out between fixed versus variable cost basis across the industry, range of products and services offered, and strategies for driving competitive differentiation.
2. *Supplier Power* factors include supplier brand reputation, supplier geographical coverage, quality of products and services, depth of key customer relationships, and ability to bid on a wide range of products and services.
3. *Buyer Power* factors include buyer choice and preferences, number and size of buyers, switching frequency and related switching costs, importance of the

product and/or service to the buyer's product value and differentiation, volume discounts, just-in-time scheduling, and products and services availability.

4. *Product and Technology Developments* factors include pricing and quality of alternative products and services, vulnerability to market distribution and sourcing changes, fashion trends, impact of legislative and government actions, and compliance risks.

5. *New Market Entrants* factors include barriers to entry, geographical and cultural factors, depth and resilience of incumbent positioning, financial and strategic feasibility for new entrants, and difficulty in establishing a maintainable presence in the market.

Figure 7-2 summarizes Porter's Five Forces Analysis.

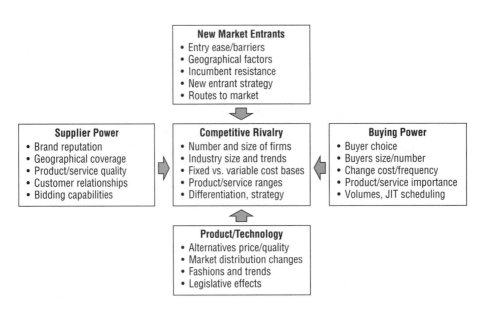

Michael E. Porter "Competitive Strategy: Techniques for Analyzing Industries and Competitors" 1980

Figure 7-2: Porter's Five Forces Analysis

Michael Porter's Value Chain Analysis

Wikipedia defines Michael Porter's Value Chain Analysis as follows:

> *A value chain is a chain of activities for a firm operating in a specific industry. The business unit is the appropriate level for construction of a value chain, not the divisional level or corporate level. Products pass through all activities of the chain in order, and at each activity the product gains some value. The chain of activities gives the products more added value than the sum of the independent activities' values.*

The Value Chain Analysis covers two categories of activities—primary activities and support activities. The primary activities are probably the most familiar, as they deal with the steps and processes necessary to take a product or service from its raw materials to final customer sale and support. The primary activities are the following:

- *Inbound Logistics* includes the identification, sourcing, procurement, and supplier management of the "raw materials" that comprise the final product or service.
- *Operations* includes the engineering, inventory management, and manufacturing of the final product or service. Note: Any technologies incorporated into the product or service are also included here.
- *Outbound Logistics* includes the logistics and distribution of the final product and service.
- *Marketing and Sales* includes the marketing, merchandising, promotions, advertising, sales, and channel management to get the completed product and service to the end customer.
- *Service* includes the support and maintenance of products and services after they are delivered to the customer.

The secondary activities are less familiar, but equally important in supporting product and service scalability:

- *Procurement* includes the acquisition of supporting maintenance, repair, and operations (MRO) materials and services.
- *Technology Development* includes the supporting technologies, both information technologies as well as other technologies, important for keeping the lights on. Technologies integrated into the product are covered in the Operations stage.

- *Human Resource Management* includes the recruiting, hiring, development, and firing of personnel.
- *Infrastructure* includes the physical infrastructure such as buildings, offices, and warehouses.

Figure 7-3 summarizes Porter's Value Chain Analysis.

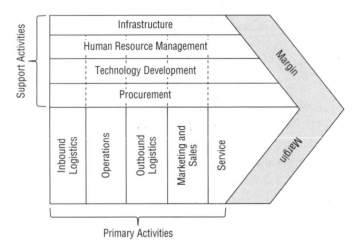

Michael E. Porter "Competitive Strategy: Techniques for Analyzing Industries and Competitors" 1980

Figure 7-3: Porter's Value Chain Analysis

Value Creation Process: Merchandising Example

Using a real-world example, you will learn how to apply the three different value creation techniques (Big Data Envisioning Worksheet, Porter's Value Chain Analysis, and Porter's Five Forces Analysis) to identify specific areas of the business where the four big data business drivers can impact the organization's key business initiative. Let's say that you are an executive at Foot Looker, a leading retailer in the men's and women's sports footwear and apparel industry with both online and brick-and-mortar presences. In Foot Locker's 2010 annual report, a letter from the company president to shareholders spells out Foot Locker's major business initiative:

> …become the Power Merchandiser of athletic footwear and apparel with clearly-defined Brand Banners.

That is, Foot Locker is looking to leverage innovative, category-defining brands, such as Nike and Under Armour, to increase store traffic, store sales, and overall profitability, which is reinforced by other strategic priorities listed in the letter:

> *Develop a compelling Apparel Assortment*
> *Make our stores and Internet sites Exciting Places to shop and buy*
> *Increase the Productivity of all of our assets*

For those readers not in the retail business, merchandising is the pricing, promotion, packaging, and placement of a product at the point of customer engagement, such as walking through a physical store, surfing a website, or using a smartphone app. Merchandising applies the four P's of the retail business—package, placement, promotion, and price—in order to drive individual product and market basket sales and margins. Merchandising's goal is to display, feature, promote, and price products—whether individually or in combination (for example, socks and shoes)—in order to drive the sale of products to a customer. Every time you walk through a retail store, visit a retail website, or open a retail smartphone app, you are being exposed to a wide variety of merchandising "treatments" to catch your attention and persuade you to purchase products.

Big Data Envisioning Worksheet: Merchandising Example

Let's start with the Big Data Envisioning Worksheet. This worksheet provides the framework against which you can apply the four big data business drivers to brainstorm specific areas where big data can impact Foot Locker's merchandising key business initiative. As outlined above, merchandising covers a wide variety of different tactics and techniques. However, for the purposes of this exercise, you're going to just focus on how you could improve customer profiling and segmentation in order to improve Foot Locker's in-store and on-site merchandising effectiveness as measured by the increase in cross-sell, up-sell, and market basket revenues and margins.

Driver #1

How would you use detailed POS transactional data to improve customer segmentation?

- You could use the detailed POS transactions, combined with Foot Locker customer loyalty data, to increase the number of customer micro-segments from 50 to 500 based on individual and market basket buying behaviors and product propensities.

- You could create more granular and tightly focused merchandising campaigns by targeting the higher-fidelity customer segments, and driving specific merchandising activities by season (for example, basketball March Madness, Super Bowl, World Series), and at the city and ZIP+4 code levels.

- You could create location-specific customer segments based on the current sports season (baseball, soccer, basketball) combined with the local sports teams' games.

Driver #2

How would you integrate unstructured data such as social media data with your structured transactional data to improve customer segmentation

- You could mine social media data to identify customers' sports-relevant interests, passions, associations, and affiliations to create richer, more targeted merchandising models.

- You could analyze social media feeds to identify which merchandising campaigns are successful and which ones are not, based on customer sentiment analysis.

- You could acquire smartphone app data from apps such as MapMyRun.com to create geography, store and sports-specific micro-segments.

Driver #3

How would you use real-time data to improve customer segmentation?

- You could update customer acquisition up-sell and cross-sell (next best offer) scores daily, while the merchandising campaign is active, based on how the different customer segments are responding to the merchandising (for example, weekend basketball warriors are responding 50 percent more than planned, but youth soccer fanatics are down 20 percent more than planned).

- You could recalculate merchandising models immediately after "significant" local sporting events (for example, the San Francisco Giants winning the World Series…again, or the Golden State Warriors making the basketball playoffs for the first time in over a decade).

- You could integrate local sports events to fine-tune in-flight merchandising campaigns (such as, taking advantage of a local professional baseball team's run for the playoffs).

Driver #4

How would you use advanced or predictive analytics to improve customer segmentation?

- You could develop analytic models that monitor and triage current merchandising campaign performance in order to recommend the "best" customer micro-segments to target given a particular merchandising campaign's audience, product, and sales goals.
- You could develop cross-media attribution modeling to optimize merchandising spending across e-mail, direct mail, web, mobile and in-store activities.

Figure 7-4 shows how the envisioning worksheet would capture the different ideas that came out of the segmentation brainstorming exercise. The brainstorming process would continue as you explore the impact of the four big data business drivers on other merchandising tactics like pricing, packaging, promotion, and product placement.

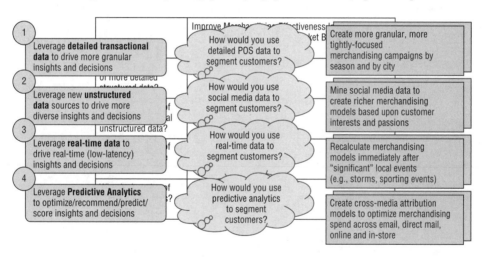

Figure 7-4: Envisioning Worksheet: Merchandising Example

Michael Porter's Value Chain Analysis: Merchandising Example

Next, let's next apply the Porter Value Chain Analysis model to the Foot Locker merchandising business initiative. You'll use the Value Chain Analysis model to identify how the four big data business drivers could impact Foot Locker's merchandising business initiative (Figure 7-5).

In the area of Inbound Logistics, you could optimize your merchandising effectiveness initiative by providing real-time POS insights via an integrated data feed

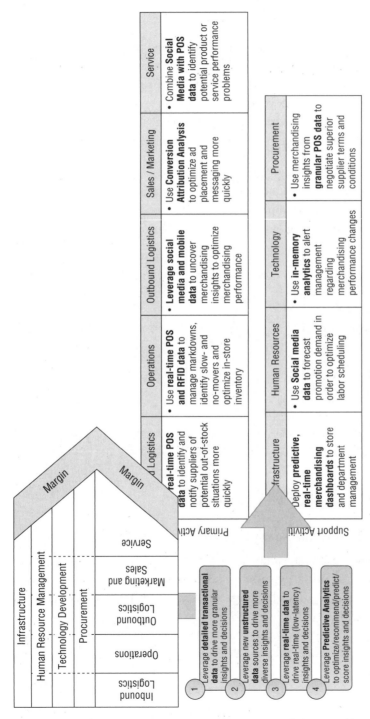

Figure 7-5: Value Chain Analysis: Merchandising Example

(API) to proactively notify suppliers of potential merchandising out-of-stock and over stock situations prior to them becoming problems.

In the area of Operations, you could optimize your merchandising effectiveness initiative by integrating real-time POS and inventory data to predict merchandise demand, manage merchandise markdowns, and identify slow- and no-movers to optimize in-store/on-site inventory.

In the area of Outbound Logistics, you could apply big data analytics to optimize your merchandising effectiveness initiative in the following ways:

- Leveraging social media and mobile data to uncover merchandising and product sentiment that could impact stock and inventory levels for active marketing campaigns
- Using analytics sandbox to model event-driven logistics impacts such as, a major league baseball game in the area or unplanned construction work on a major travel artery

In the area of Marketing and Sales, you could optimize your merchandising effectiveness initiative by using conversion attribution analysis across search, display, mobile, and social media to optimize web display and mobile ad placement, keyword bids, and messaging more quickly.

In the area of Service, you could optimize your merchandising effectiveness initiative by combining social media data with your customer loyalty data to create more frequent, higher-fidelity customer scores for customer areas such as retention, fraud, up-sell/cross-sell, and net promoter.

These tactics are summarized in Figure 7-6.

	Inbound Logistics	Operations	Outbound Logistics	Sales / Marketing	Service
Primary Activities	• Use **real-time POS data** to identify and notify suppliers of potential out-of-stock situations more quickly	• Use **real-time POS and RFID data** to manage markdowns, identify slow- and no-movers and optimize in-store inventory	• **Leverage social media and mobile data** to uncover merchandising insights to optimize merchandising performance	• Use **Conversion Attribution Analysis** to optimize ad placement and messaging more quickly	• Combine **Social Media with POS data** to identify potential product or service performance problems

	Infrastructure	Human Resources	Technology	Procurement
Support Activities	• Deploy **predictive, real-time merchandising dashboards** to store and department management	• Use **Social media data** to forecast promotion demand in order to optimize labor scheduling	• Use **in-memory analytics** to alert management regarding merchandising performance changes	• Use merchandising insights from **granular POS data** to negotiate superior supplier terms and conditions

Figure 7-6: Value Chain Analysis: Merchandising Example

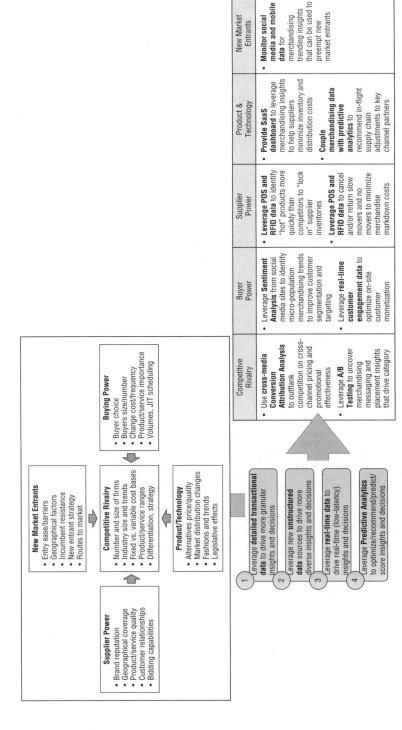

Figure 7-7: Five Forces Analysis: Merchandising Example

The Porter Value Chain Analysis provides a business-centric approach to looking at how big data could potentially impact your organization's internal value creation processes. This inside-out business valuation perspective facilitates collaboration with your line-of-business (LOB) stakeholders to help them envision the realm of possibilities with respect to big data.

Michael Porter's Five Forces Analysis: Merchandising Example

Finally, let's apply the Porter Five Forces Analysis model to the Foot Locker merchandising business initiative. We'll use the Five Forces outside-in Analysis model to identify how the four big data business drivers could impact Foot Locker's merchandising effectiveness initiative, as summarized in Figure 7-7.

In the area of *Competitive Rivalry,* you could apply big data to your merchandising effectiveness initiative to drive competitive advantage in the following ways:

- Using cross-media Conversion Attribution Analysis across search, display, social, and mobile advertising to outflank competition on cross-channel pricing, placement, and promotional effectiveness
- Leveraging A/B testing to uncover merchandising messaging and placement insights that drive category market share growth and increased shopping occurrence profitability

In the area of Buyer Power, you could apply big data to your merchandising effectiveness initiative to uncover unique market, product, and customer insights to counter the growing power of buyers and buying coalitions, including:

- Leveraging Sentiment Analysis from social media sites to identify and quantify micro-population merchandising trends and insights to improve customer segmentation, targeting, pricing, and packaging effectiveness
- Leveraging real-time customer sales and CRM, web and mobile engagement data to optimize active or in-flight merchandise targeting to increase on-site customer monetization (for example, to increase conversion rates, and to increase up-sell and cross-sell effectiveness)

■ Leveraging recommendation engines to improve the customer experience (as measured by net promoter scores, repeat purchases, and loyalty), optimize merchandising margins, and minimize merchandising markdowns

In the area of Supplier Power, you could apply big data to your merchandising effectiveness initiative to glean unique market, product, and customer insights to counter the growing power of suppliers, including:

■ Leveraging detailed POS and inventory data to identify "hot" products more quickly than competitors in order to "lock in" supplier inventories and favorable terms and conditions

■ Leveraging detailed POS and RFID data to cancel and/or return slow movers and no movers faster than competitors in order to minimize merchandise markdown and inventory carrying costs

In the area of Product and Technology Innovation, you could apply big data to your merchandising effectiveness initiative to identify areas where products and/or technology can be used to drive buyer or supplier lock-in, or to create barriers to entry for new market entrants, including:

■ Providing a software-as-a-service dashboard and predictive analytics platform for your key partners and suppliers that leverages merchandising data and insights to help suppliers minimize their procurement, inventory, and distribution costs

■ Coupling merchandising data with predictive analytics capabilities to recommend in-process supply chain and inventory adjustments to your key channel and distribution partners

In the area of New Market Entrants, you could use big data to identify and preempt market opportunities before new market entrants can gain a foothold. For example, constantly monitoring social media and mobile data for merchandising trending insights that can be used to preempt new market entrants.

These approaches are summarized in the following list:

Five Forces Analysis: Merchandising Example

- **Competitive Rivalry:**
  - Use cross-media Conversion Attribution Analysis to outflank competition on cross-channel pricing and promotional effectiveness.
  - Leverage A/B Testing to uncover merchandising messaging and placement insights that drive category.
- **Buyer Power:**
  - Leverage Sentiment Analysis from social media sites to identify micro-population merchandising trends to improve customer segmentation and targeting.
  - Leverage real-time customer engagement data to optimize on-site customer monetization.
- **Supplier Power:**
  - Leverage POS and data to identify "hot" products more quickly than competitors to "lock in" supplier inventories.
  - Leverage POS and data to cancel and/or return slow-movers and no-movers to minimize merchandise markdown costs.
- **Product & Technology:**
  - Provide SaaS dashboard to leverage merchandising insights to help suppliers minimize inventory and distribution costs.
  - Couple merchandising data with predictive analytics to recommend in-flight supply chain adjustments to key channel partners.
- **New Market Entrants:**
  - Monitor social media and mobile data for merchandising trending insights that can be used to preempt new market entrants.

The Porter Five Forces Analysis provides a business-centric approach to looking at the potential of your big data initiative from the framework of how it could impact the forces and players that define your marketplace. This "outside-in" business valuation perspective facilitates collaboration between the IT and business stakeholders to envision the realm of possibilities with big data, and to gain early buy-in to support the organization's big data initiative.

Summary

This chapter provided several detailed, hands-on techniques for leveraging big data to impact your value creation processes. You were introduced to the four big data business drivers:

1. Access to more detailed, structured, transactional (dark) data
2. Access to internal and external unstructured data
3. Real-time or low-latency access to data
4. Integrating predictive analytics into your key business processes

You worked through several generic examples across different industries to comprehend of how the four big data business drivers could impact the business.

This chapter then introduced the Big Data Envisioning Worksheet as a tool for brainstorming how the four big data business drivers could be applied to a specific business initiative. You walked through several business examples—predictive maintenance, customer satisfaction, and customer micro-segmentation—where you applied the four big data business drivers to identify areas of the business where big data could impact an organization's value creation processes.

Next, you were introduced to Michael Porter's Value Chain Analysis and Five Forces Analysis as two additional value creation frameworks that you can use to ascertain how the four big data business drivers could be applied to a specific business initiative.

Finally, you walked through a real-world example of how Foot Locker could leverage the four big data business drivers and the three different value creation models—Big Data Envisioning Worksheet, Porter's Value Chain Analysis, and Porter's Five Forces Analysis—to improve their merchandising effectiveness initiative.

All in all, I hope that this chapter felt like an introduction to the Big Data MBA.

8

Big Data User Experience Ramifications

In Chapter 5, we talked about the ramifications of big data on the internal business stakeholder's user interface. We discussed how integrating predictive analytics into your key business processes, coupled with new unstructured data sources and real-time (low-latency) data feeds, facilitated the transformation of the user interface to lead with relevant insights and actionable recommendations. Instead of delivering a traditional business intelligence user interface with a multitude of charts and graphics and the promise of "slicing and dicing," instead we can leverage big data capabilities to tease out and deliver only those insights (and corresponding recommendations) that are of interest to the business stakeholders and material to the business.

This chapter will now focus on leveraging those same insights to transform our customers' or consumers' user experience; to look external to our organization to determine how to leverage big data to deliver a more compelling and more sticky user experience.

As previously discussed in the data monetization stage of the Big Data Business Model Maturity Index, the customer and product insights that can be mined from big data can have a dramatic impact on your customers' user experience. The opportunity to leverage insights about each customer's behavioral tendencies, coupled with insights about "similar" customers' behavioral tendencies, can be a source of valuable, relevant, and actionable insights for your customers. As a result of these insights, you can create a more engaging, actionable, and ultimately more profitable relationship with your customers.

Let's start this chapter with an example of what *not* to do with respect to leveraging (or not leveraging) insights about your customers.

The Unintelligent User Experience

Most organizations don't spend enough time and energy trying to understand what their customers want to accomplish. That is, what are the objectives or results that your customers are trying to obtain? This lack of knowledge about your customers' objectives can result in an unintelligent user experience. This is a problem caused by the lack of commitment and effort by organizations to fully understand what their customers are trying to accomplish, which is different than what the customer may actually be doing. If you don't completely understand your customers' objectives and what they are trying to accomplish, then you have little chance of delivering a user experience that will be beneficial, meaningful, and actionable for your customers. This user experience challenge is only exacerbated by big data and the growing expectations by your customers that you do something beneficial with all the data that you are gathering about them.

Here is a real-world example of how *not* to leverage data and analytics to provide relevant engagement with your customers. My daughter received the e-mail shown in Figure 8-1 from our cell phone provider warning her that she was about to exceed her monthly data usage limit of 2 GB. She was very concerned that she was about to go over her data limit and it would start costing her (actually, costing me) a significant but undisclosed amount of money. (Note: The circled "Monday, August 13, 2012" date in the figure will play an important role later in this example.)

Figure 8-1: How not to leverage data and analytics to provide relevant engagement with customers

The part of the e-mail message that most concerned and upset my daughter was:

> *Our systems have detected that you are nearing your data plan limit.*
> *Your base plan has a monthly allowance of 20 GB. Any data usage which*
> *exceeds your plan allowance will be billed at $10 per each additional*
> *1 GB.*

I asked my daughter what information she would need in order to make decisions about altering her cell phone usage (in particular, her posting of photos and videos with Facebook, Instagram, Vine, and Snapchat, which are the biggest data hog culprits in her case) so that she would not exceed her data plan limits. She came up with the following questions that she would need to answer:

- How much of my data plan do I have left?
- When does my new monthly data usage plan restart?
- At my current usage rate, when will I run over for this period?

Understanding the Key Decisions to Build a Relevant User Experience

The data plan e-mail example highlights a three-step process that all organizations can employ to identify the relevant information that customers need in order to be able to improve the effectiveness of their interactions and engagements with your organization. This process is:

1. Understand your customers' objectives for engaging with your organization—what they are trying to accomplish in their interactions with your organization (in this example, interact with friends and families while not exceeding my monthly data usage plan). The bottom line is understanding why your customers use your product or service (or the corollary, why *should* customers use your product or service).

2. Capture the decisions that your customers need to make with respect to their objectives in order to improve the effectiveness of their interactions with your organization and your products and services (for instance, alter app usage behaviors).

3. Identify what information the users need in order to support the decisions that they need to make. In our example, the customer might ask: How much of my data plan do I have left? When does my new month start? When will I run over for my current period?

Understanding the relationship between your customer's engagement objectives, decisions, and information needs is the foundation for creating a beneficial, meaningful, and actionable user experience. That user experience could then provide the right information (and eventually recommendations) in the right content to the right customer to make the right decisions at the right time.

So to continue the cellular provider story, I went online to research my daughter's key questions. Here are the answers I was able to uncover after much exploration:

- How much of my data plan do I have left? Current usage as of August 13, 2012, was 65%.
- When does my new month start? In one day (monthly data usage counter restarts on August 14, 2012).
- At my current usage rate, when will I run over for this month? *Never!*

Given the results of my analysis, my daughter did not have anything to worry about regarding her monthly data usage plan. She would have to consume nearly as much bandwidth in her final 24 hours (assuming that she does not sleep) as she had already consumed over the previous 30 days. The probability of that happening was near zero (or the same probability of me beating Usain Bolt in the 100-meter dash). The bottom line is that the cellular provider should have never sent the e-mail warning since it had no value or relevance, and only succeeded in adding to my daughter's anxiety and making it much more likely for me to start looking for a new cellular provider.

Using Big Data Analytics to Improve Customer Engagement

Let's say the situation was different and there was a significant probability that my daughter was going to exceed her monthly data usage plan. Then our cellular company could have provided a user experience that included the information necessary to help her make a decision about data usage behaviors. The user experience could have looked something Figure 8-2:

This sample e-mail has all the information my daughter would need to make a data usage decision, including:

- Actual usage to date (82%)
- A forecast of usage by the end of the plan period (118%)
- Current data and monthly data usage plan reset (September 1)
- The cost of going over the usage limit ($20)

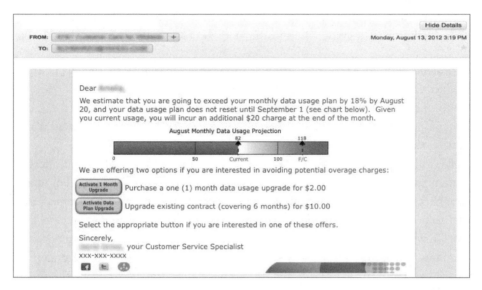

Figure 8-2: A better example of how to leverage data and analytics to provide relevant engagement with customers

Our cellular company could implement an analytic process that calculates, daily, the likelihood that each subscriber's data usage will end up in the red zone (projected data usage greater than 90% of the monthly data usage plan) before the end of the usage period. The cellular provider would then have the information necessary to make an intelligent decision about whether or not to send the e-mail warning.

With this information, my daughter is now in a position to make an "intelligent" decision. In fact, our cellular company could leverage insights about my daughter's usage patterns, tendencies, and trends to take the user experience to the next level. The e-mail could not only alert the subscriber to the potential problem, but could also recommend some specific usage changes, such as:

- We notice that you use Facebook, Instagram, Vine, and Snapchat frequently. Using a WiFi connection more often could reduce your network data usage.
- We noticed that you keep over 30 apps running in the GPS tracking mode. We recommend that you turn off the tracking for those apps that you use infrequently, such as Google Maps, Ms. Pacman, Safari, Chrome, Urban Outfitters, and A&F. Click *here* to learn how to turn off the GPS tracking in these apps.

In fact, the cellular provider could go one step further and make it easier for the subscriber to take action to avoid potential overage by presenting a couple of "one click to activate" options, such as:

- Click *here* to purchase a one-month (1) data usage upgrade for $2.00.
- Click *here* to upgrade your existing contract (covering 6 months) for $10.00.

The cellular provider has now provided everything the subscriber needs to know to reduce the potential overage probability, as well as presented a couple of relevant, easy-to-understand purchase options to avoid the onerous overage charges. The cellular company has converted a bothersome situation into a win-win for everyone. But wait, there's more!

The cellular provider is now in a position to experiment with different offers to different subscribers to optimize the pricing and packaging of the different offers. The ability to *instrument* these offers (to measure offer response effectiveness) and *experiment* with different offers (to see which offers appeal to which subscriber segments in what situations) puts the cellular provider on the path to not only becoming a more predictive enterprise, but also puts them in a position to leverage their analytics and insights to provide a more complete and compelling user experience.

This cellular provider is not alone in missing opportunities to leverage the data they know about their customers in order to provide a more relevant and meaningful customer experience. Organizations capture a lot of data about their customers and their buying and usage patterns, but little of that data is being mined in order to create the insights needed to improve the user experience. Big data will only exacerbate this problem, and organizations will either learn to jump on big data as an opportunity to improve their user experience, or they will get buried by the data and continue to provide irrelevant customer engagements.

Uncovering and Leveraging Customer Insights

One of the most important business drivers of big data is the novel insights that organizations can gather about their customers' behaviors, tendencies, and propensities, and how those insights can rewire an organization's customer value creation processes. Your customers, through their interactions on the web, activity on social media sites, and use of their smartphone apps, are leaving their digital fingerprints all over the Internet (see Figure 8-3).

Figure 8-3: How Much Data is Created Every Minute? (Domo Infographic)

Source: http://www.domo.com/blog/2012/06/how-much-data-is-created-every-minute/

These digital fingerprints provide invaluable insights into their areas of interests (their areas of "likes"), passions (areas of advocacy and promoter status), associations (the formal groups to which they belong), and affiliations (those causes in which they believe), and can be leveraged to improve every customer engagement point. These customer insights can impact every point in your customer lifecycle engagement process—from how you profile and segment, to how you up-sell and cross-sell, to how you drive advocacy.

Rewiring Your Customer Lifecycle Management Processes

Unfortunately, organizations don't tend to think about the entirety of their customer lifecycle process. Many organizations have separate marketing groups focused on spot solutions for areas such as acquisition, up-sell, retention, and advocacy. For example, many organizations are fanatically focused on reducing their churn rate, or the rate at which existing customers leave or attrite from being an active customer. It is estimated that it costs 10 times more to acquire a new customer than it does to retain an existing one, which makes this a reasonable area on which to focus. Organizations expend a significant amount of marketing, sales, and support resources in an effort to identify potential churn or attrition candidates and take correction actions early enough in the customer engagement process to prevent the customers from churning or leaving.

However, I'd challenge that an organization's churn rate numbers are even worse than they think—that they don't consider the money and resources wasted in profiling, segmenting, targeting, and acquiring the wrong prospects, and the ineffectiveness and waste in making the wrong offers to the wrong customers in an effort to up-sell and cross-sell them. And let's not even get started on the lack of understanding about advocacy development. In reality, there is customer churn, or defections, at each step in the customer lifecycle engagement process (see Figure 8-4).

The key challenge is how will your organization leverage customer insights to optimize all the customer engagement points that comprise the customer engagement lifecycle. Organizations need to couple their existing customer demographic and product purchase data with usage behaviors (tendencies, propensities, trends), and social activities (customer's interests, passions, associations, affiliations) to uncover and actionable insights about their individual customers. Organizations need to integrate these new customer insights to drive critical financial metrics such as customer's lifetime value (LTV) and customer's likelihood to recommend (LTR).

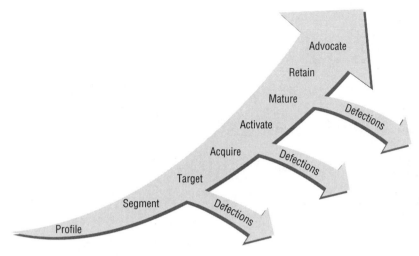

Figure 8-4: Optimize your customer engagement lifecycle

To do this, organizations need to become much more proficient at instrumenting every customer touch point, including social media, mobile apps, and human (sales, service, and support) interactions. Organizations also need to embrace experimentation as a means to learn even more about their customers—to understand which messaging, promotions, and offers customers respond to, and which ones they do not. Organizations need to appreciate that every customer engagement is an opportunity to learn more about that individual customer, which ultimately affects the quality and relevance of the customer engagement and the long-term profitability to the organization.

Using Customer Insights to Drive Business Profitability

Optimizing the customer lifecycle engagement processes is probably the number one big data business opportunity for organizations in the business-to-consumer (B2C) space. This includes companies such as retailers, banks and credit unions, credit card companies, insurance companies, cellular providers, cable or digital TV providers, healthcare providers, and healthcare payers. A study done by R. S. Kaplan and S. Anderson in 2004 discovered that, generally speaking, across all industries (see Figure 8-5):

- 0 to 25% of customers drive greater than 100% of profits
- 50 to 60% deliver no profits
- 10 to 25% deliver negative profits

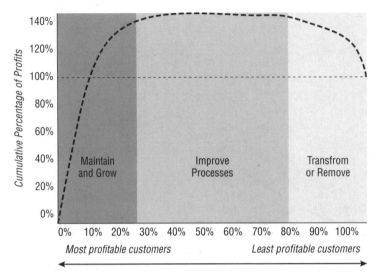

Figure 8-5: Customer profitability curve
Source: R. S. Kaplan and S. Anderson, "Time-driven Activity-based Costing," Harvard Business Review (November 2004)

This implies that if you could "fire" the 75 to 90 percent of your non-profitable customers, you would not only increase profitability, you would also dramatically reduce your overall cost structure for targeting, acquiring, and retaining unprofitable customers.

Since it is not realistic for an organization to fire all of their non-profitable customers, organizations need to dramatically improve their ability to understand and quantify the characteristics, behaviors, propensities, interests, passions, associations, and affiliations of their customer and prospect bases in order to:

- Move customers into the more profitable part of the relationship curve.
- Develop plans, programs, and offerings that can service unprofitable customers in a more cost-effective manner.

The financial value of developing a deep understanding of each of your customers—their behaviors, propensities, interests, passions, associations, and affiliations—in order to optimize the entire customer engagement lifecycle can be seen from the overwhelming business value of retaining key customers and building advocacy and likelihood to recommend (see Figure 8-6).

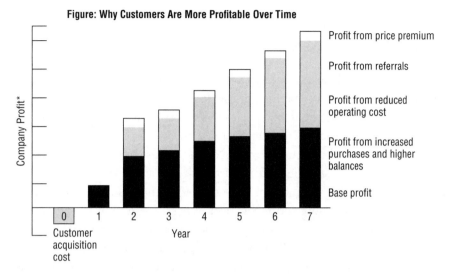

Figure: Why Customers Are More Profitable Over Time

Figure 8-6: Customer retention business driver
Source: "The Service Profit Chain" Heskett, Sasser, and Schlesinger 1997

This study highlights the key business drivers that make the retention of key customers so critical to the long-term viability of businesses. These business value drivers are:

- Base profits from initial product purchases, product replacements, and servicing of the basic product
- Additional profits from product and service cross-sell and up-sell opportunities—that is, marketing to your existing customers, or your "install base"
- Increased profitability by eliminating customer acquisition costs
- Profits from referrals (which in 1997 might have been a smaller opportunity that it is in today's social media-crazed world of referrals, net promoters, and advocacy)
- Profit from price premium that some customers are willing to pay in order to avoid having to switch to another product; leverage the inertia of most customers to stay with their status quo, even through relatively minor price increases because it's still more expensive to switch than it is to just pay the higher prices

Big Data Can Power a New Customer Experience

One of the more powerful big data monetization opportunities is to leverage all the customer, product, and operational insights buried in big data to radically rethink and improve the nature of the customer relationship. We can see from the figures earlier in the chapter that the timely and relevant application of customer insights at the segment and individual customer level can drive increased profitability, loyalty, and advocacy of your "most important" customers. And many of these relevant, meaningful, and actionable insights can be presented to the customers via a more relevant, meaningful, and more actionable user experience. Let's walk through a couple of examples—one for the business-to-consumer (B2C) organizations and one for the business-to-business (B2B) organizations—of how organizations can leverage customer, product, and operational insights to provide a new, more compelling customer user experience.

B2C Example: Powering the Retail Customer Experience

Let's start with a retail example (since most readers have some personal experience with the retail industry). Much like how financial services organizations (e.g., Mint, which is a free service that integrates your bank, credit card, investment, and loan transactions, as well as create personalized budgets and goals, all through a consistent web and mobile experience) have been working to become strategic financial advisors to their customers, retailers could put themselves in a similar position by helping shoppers optimize their shopping budgets given the customers' shopping, meal, and budget objectives. Let's create a couple of simple mockups to help drive home the customer experience potential.

Today shoppers receive a shopping receipt like the one shown on the left side of Figure 8-7. The shopping receipt tells shoppers what they purchased, the quantity of each item purchased, the price of each item, and total money spent. In some cases, the receipt also tells shoppers how much they saved using their customer loyalty card, and maybe even things like how many credits they have earned for a free coffee, for example. The receipt is really nothing more than an audit trail of what they purchased.

Instead of this traditional sales receipt, what if the sales receipt becomes more of a shopping optimization dashboard, like the image shown on the right side of Figure 8-7? What if you leveraged the customer's historical purchase data and shopping tendencies to provide a spending report much like what financial services companies provide to their customers? Such an updated user experience could provide some of the following shopping insights:

- Highlight the shoppers' purchase trends across types of products and product categories, and the frequency of those purchases, by season.
- Provide benchmarks against similar shoppers' buying preferences across different product categories, stores, and holiday events.
- Provide Amazon-like product recommendations to make specific product or service recommendations.
- Provide insights and specific recommendations to help customers optimize their shopping budgets given their shopping, meal, and budget objectives.

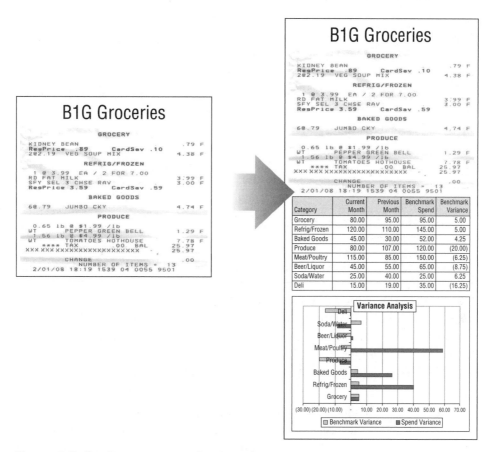

Figure 8-7: Retail customer experience mockup

Now let's take this mockup one step further. Let's look at how we might leverage all of the retailer's customer loyalty and shopping data to transform a retailer's smartphone app into a "shopping advisor."

We've enhanced the retailer's smartphone app to include a "Grocery Budget Analysis" option (see the button at the bottom of the smartphone app shown in Figure 8-8). This updated smartphone app goes a big step further by helping

shoppers optimize their shopping budget by delivering personalized shopping recommendations (given their particular shopping objectives and budget constraints)
and even the potential to deliver real-time product offers.

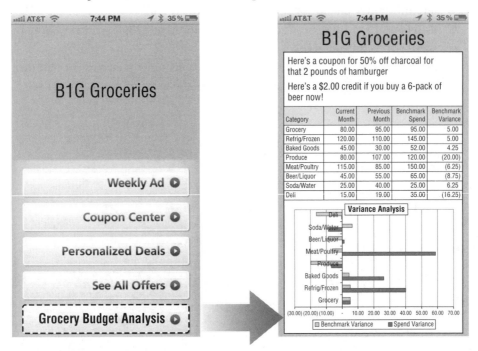

Figure 8-8: Mobile apps drive customer experience

Clicking on the "Grocery Budget Analysis" button would open a module that not
only shows the shopper's purchasing trends, but could also provide insights into that
shopper's buying preferences versus a benchmark group to identify ways that the
shopper could spend their budgets more effectively. The module could also provide
specific budget, product, and meal suggestions, such as, "You seem to buy lots of
Cap'n Crunch. Purchase three boxes and get 50% off the regular price."

The purpose of this mockup is to get the business owners to start "what if'ing"
the types of insights they might be able to glean from this expanded access to more
data about their customers and their product preferences, and how they could
present such insights in a way that creates a more compelling and differentiated
customer experience. Some of the types of questions that the business owners might
contemplate could include:

- What sort of monetization opportunities can I uncover if I had access to my
  customers' potential purchase behaviors, tendencies, and patterns by customer
  segment?

- What sort of promotions and recommendations could I generate if I had the ability to combine a customer's purchase history with seasonal holidays and local events?
- What services could I provide if I could capture my customers' current purchase activities in real-time while they are still in the store?
- What sort of promotional opportunities are there if I could easily access and compare the purchase behaviors and propensities of similar customers' market basket purchases?
- How could I leverage customer purchase patterns and behaviors to deliver customer-specific offers and shopping insights during their in-store experience?

The traditional brick-and-mortar retail industry is ready to challenge the online retailers' ability to affect the customer's real-time shopping activity with their own in-store recommendations and insights that will improve the customer's shopping experience. Not content to be just another channel, big data, new technology, and analytic developments in the retail industry hold the potential to transform customer engagement from a tactical purchase occurrence into a strategic, long-lasting relationship. Helping shoppers optimize their budget and improve their shopping experience will create a "sticky" relationship that draws them back to the retailer time and time again.

B2B Example: Powering Small- and Medium-Sized Merchant Effectiveness

Likewise for B2B organizations, there are opportunities to leverage customer, product, and operational insights to improve the effectiveness and profitability of your key customers. Let's say that you are a digital marketplace that helps small- and medium-sized merchants sell their products. Your average customer likely does not have the same data management and analysis capabilities as your organization, yet they are highly dependent on your marketplace for the long-term viability of their business.

What if you were able to capture all of your business customers' transactional data (through a data exchange and increased digital instrumentation) and could use that data, coupled with advanced analytics, to help your business customers improve their overall business performance? You could create an entirely new customer experience by creating an *intelligent* merchant dashboard that helps the merchants:

- Improve campaign marketing effectiveness
- Improve online product merchandising effectiveness
- Optimize marketing media mix spend
- Optimize product pricing
- Optimize merchandise markdown management
- Reduce inventory and supply chain costs

You could also leverage insights from other merchants to provide market performance insights (marketing, campaign, and financial performance benchmarks, market share, share of voice, and share of wallet) by product categories. You could leverage the analysis of competitive markets and product category performance to make recommendations to merchants on how they could improve their business performance (see Figure 8-9).

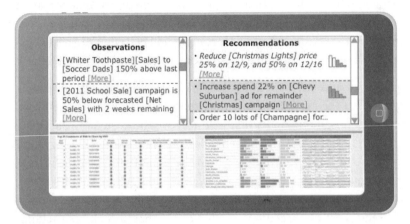

Figure 8-9: Mobile apps drive customer/partner experience

You could even provide recommendations to merchants regarding what actions they could take to improve business performance. You could provide recommendations for each of the key business decisions the merchant needs to make in areas such as merchandising, marketing, and inventory management.

This intelligent merchant dashboard mockup is designed for business users who are not analysts. The mockup is designed for business users who need the data and the analytics to tell them what's going on in their business, to uncover useful and material insights buried in the data across the key business dimensions of customers, products, and campaigns, and to provide recommendations as to the actions the merchant could take to improve their business performance. The merchant dashboard provides two key pieces of information in support of those business user requirements:

1. Insights, which are observations—both problems and opportunities—of unusual business occurrences uncovered in the data. These insights need to

be of significant business value to warrant the business users investing their time and effort to investigate the insight.

2. Recommendations, which are actions or decisions that the merchant can make to help them improve their business performance.

Both the insights and the recommendations could have a "More Detail" link that opens up another window that provides the data and analytics that support that specific insight or recommendation. The recommendations in this mockup also provide a "strength of the recommendation" indicator that quickly shows the merchant the estimated effectiveness of this recommendation based on historical performance (calculated by analyzing the historical effectiveness of that recommendation from similar merchants who have accepted that recommendation).

Recommendations also provide an opportunity to capture additional insights about your merchants and the effectiveness of the analytic model. Instrumentation of the recommendations through the use of pull-down menus can be used to capture the following additional information:

- What recommendations did the merchant "Accept" and what was the performance of that recommendation?
- What recommendations did the merchant "Reject" and why did the merchant reject that particular recommendation (for example, was it not relevant or not actionable)?

This additional information can be used to improve the analytic modeling effectiveness by capturing the results of the recommendation and using those results to fine-tune the supporting analytic model, while improving the overall merchant user experience by providing only recommendations that are relevant, material, and effective to that merchant.

The key to successfully leveraging big data to impact the user experience is to provide the data and insights necessary to help the business users identify what's driving business performance and what actions they could take to improve their performance. For the digital marketplace example, the dashboard needs to provide insights and recommendations that support the following business user questions and decisions (Table 8-1):

Table 8-1: The Intelligent Merchant Dashboard

Business Users Ask...	Intelligent Dashboard Delivers...
How am I performing? How do I compare to what I did last time? In what areas am I over-performing? In what areas am I under-performing?	**Business Performance Insights** Compare merchant's marketing, merchandising and inventory performance to previous periods and campaigns
What do I need to know? What should I be doing? What should I stop doing? How can I improve campaign, merchandising, and inventory performance?	**Actionable Recommendations** Prove merchandising, marketing, and inventory recommendations leveraging cross-industry best practices
What can I learn about my customers? Which customer segments are responding? Which customers are not responding? Are there other audiences I should target?	**Customer Insights** Provide insights about customer segments including demographics, behavioral tendencies, and product preferences
How am I doing versus competition? In what areas do I underperform against competitors? In what areas do I overperform against competitors?	**Competitive Insights** Provide merchant and category benchmarks to understand and improve business performance

In the next chapter, we will look at how user experience mockups can be used to drive the business envisioning process.

Summary

This chapter introduced you to the "unintelligent" user experience. Many organizations do not take advantage of the volumes of data they have captured about their customers—through initiatives like customer loyalty programs—to uncover customer and product insights that could power a more relevant and meaningful customer experience. Organizations that don't take the time to learn, understand, and leverage those customer and product insights risk delivering irrelevant, confusing, and even frustrating user experiences that in the long-run damage the organization's brand and decrease customer satisfaction and loyalty.

I defined a simple, pragmatic technique for identifying the information necessary to ensure a relevant, meaningful, and actionable user experience. The methodology ensures that your organization is providing the relevant data and insights to help your customers make the "right" decisions in their interactions with your organization.

Next, you considered how to leverage big data to improve your customer engagement processes. I discussed the importance of identifying where and how to apply big data through the entirety of your customer lifecycle process—from profiling, segmentation, targeting, acquisition, maturation, retention, and advocacy. Your organization has the opportunity to leverage customer and product insights to rewire your customer engagement processes which will improve customer profitability and drive long-term customer loyalty, as well as nurture customer advocacy.

Finally, you looked at a couple of mockups that demonstrate how your organization can leverage relevant, meaningful, and actionable insights to improve the customer experience. The mockups provided examples of how your organization can leverage insights and recommendations gleaned from big data sources to increase the value and "stickiness" of your customers' relationships with your organization.

9

Identifying Big Data Use Cases

Big data is about business transformation. I've made this point pretty clear thus far throughout the book. As discussed several times, big data can help the business stakeholders optimize their existing business processes and uncover new monetization opportunities. Big data is unlike most IT initiatives in that it requires a close and on-going collaboration with the business stakeholders to ensure that whatever is being developed and delivered is relevant and material to the business. Unlike traditional enterprise resource management (ERP) and customer relationship management (CRM) types of IT projects which can be executed with limited business stakeholder engagement, a big data project, especially one that is targeting business transformation, requires more than just business stakeholder involvement—a big data project requires deep and on-going business stakeholder *leadership*.

How do business and IT stakeholders collaborate to identify the right business opportunity upon which to focus the big data initiative, and then design the right architecture to exploit these big data monetization opportunities? How do you ensure the successful deployment of these new big data capabilities given the historically high rate of failure for the adoption of new technologies?

This chapter will introduce a tried and proven methodology—the *vision workshop*—that is based on the simple premise that business opportunities must drive big data adoption. While a technology-led approach is useful for helping an organization gain insights into what a new technology such as Hadoop can do, it is critical that the business opportunities drive the "why," "how," and "where" to implement these new big data technologies in order to achieve business stakeholder adoption and business success.

The biggest challenge with most big data projects is identifying *where* and *how* to start the big data journey. These selections are complicated by the fact that most business users (as well as most IT leaders) have a hard time envisioning the realm of what's possible with respect to leveraging new sources of big data (social, mobile, logs, telemetry, sensor, and others) and new big data technology innovations (Hadoop, MapReduce, NoSQL, and others).

Leveraging the big data envisioning techniques introduced in Chapter 7, you are now in a position to conduct the envisioning exercises, ideally as part of a larger facilitated workshop that has the following benefits:

- Ensures that your big data initiative is focused on the right business opportunities that optimally balance the trade-off between business benefit and implementation feasibility.
- Builds the organizational consensus necessary for success by aligning business and IT resources around a common set of business goals, assumptions, priorities, and metrics.
- Provides a set of metrics against which the big data initiative's success and progress will be measured.
- Reduces the likelihood of failure by identifying up-front the implementation risks of the big data initiative.

The Big Data Envisioning Process

The envisioning process, which is called the vision workshop, defines where and how big data and advanced analytics can be deployed to transform your business. The vision workshop process typically capstones in a facilitated, half-day ideation workshop that leverages group dynamics and the envisioning techniques introduced in Chapter 7 to tease out and prioritize the big data business opportunities. The workshop process does this by helping the business and IT stakeholders envision the "realm of the possible" with respect to new big data sources and new big data technologies. The vision workshop process is comprised of the following steps (see Figure 9-1):

1. Research and interviews to understand the targeted business initiative or business process
2. Data preparation and client-specific analytics development
3. Envisioning exercises to convey the "realm of the possible"
4. Brainstorm and prioritize big data use cases
5. Capture implementation risks and business value drivers

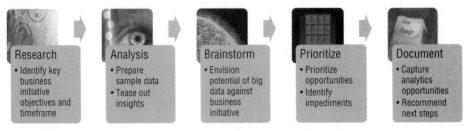

Figure 9-1: The Big Data Envisioning Process

Let's look at each of these big data envisioning steps in more detail.

Step 1: Research Business Initiatives

Prior to the facilitated ideation workshop, the business and IT teams need to identify the targeted business opportunity, challenge, or initiative upon which to focus the vision workshop. Here are some business initiative examples:

- Leverage subscriber behavioral insights to reduce churn rate and optimize customer engagement points.
- Leverage predictive analytics to improve turbine maintenance predictability and reduce unplanned maintenance.
- Leverage in-store behavioral patterns combined with customer historical purchases to power location-based offers.
- Leverage internal and external customer communications data to flag service and product problem areas and improve customer satisfaction levels.
- Leverage real-time student test results, combined with historical student test performance data, to dynamically measure student learning effectiveness.
- Leverage patient health and lifestyle data to improve hospital and care readmissions predictability.

With the targeted business initiative established, the facilitation team now gets engaged. The facilitation team is typically comprised of a lead facilitator who understands the processes and techniques for driving a group brainstorming process and facilitating consensus and prioritization amongst the workshop participants. Other key members of the facilitation team include a subject matter expert, someone who has deep experience in the industry or business function being targeted, and a data scientist, who can determine the appropriate data enrichment, analytic modeling techniques, and evaluate other potential sources of data.

The facilitation team knows what business stakeholders to engage and what data will need to be acquired, given the targeted business initiative, to fuel the ideation exercises. It is critical that the vision workshop has a well-defined scope in order to keep the exercise focused and on-track. Without a well-defined scope, the vision workshop process could easily get overwhelmed trying to satisfy the personal agendas of too many executives and too diverse business functions. Trust me when I say that focus is good, especially as you look for the "right" place to start the big data journey.

After the facilitation team has gained consensus on the vision workshop scope (targeted business initiative) and business and IT participants have been finalized, the facilitation team should research the targeted business initiative and collect relevant background information. Research should include reviewing the company's annual and quarterly financial reports, listening to analyst calls, and conducting web searches on the topic. This will not only yield insights into the organization's targeted business initiative, but could also yield insights into what competitors are doing in the same space.

The team should then interview the selected business and IT participants to:

- Capture the targeted initiative's business objectives and financial goals
- Understand how success will be measured
- Capture key business questions and decisions that must be made in support of the targeted business initiative
- Isolate current challenges
- Identify key performance indicators and critical success factors
- Review the organization's previous experience in addressing this initiative

These interviews may be face-to-face or over the phone, depending on interviewee schedules, resource availability, and timing, but face-to-face is always the preferred way to conduct the interviews.

Sample reports and spreadsheets should be gathered from the interviewees in the process. The team should spend time during the interview to understand how the business users are using and analyzing their existing reports and dashboards. Take time with the business users to understand:

- What they look for when they review a report or a dashboard
- How they know that they have a problem or opportunity
- What steps they take when they find a problem or opportunity
- What additional data or analysis they conduct to further understand the problem or opportunity
- What other stakeholders they typically engage to help analyze the problem or opportunity
- What decisions they may make based on their analysis
- Who the downstream stakeholders are—the recipients of the analysis

The facilitation team should especially take note if the business users are downloading the report data into a spreadsheet like Microsoft Excel or a personal database like Microsoft Access. They should invest the time to understand not only why the business users are downloading this data, but capture the types of analysis they are performing in the spreadsheet or personal database. Also the team should investigate if the business user is integrating other data into the analysis. These download situations provide a gold mine of insights into what the user is looking for in the data, how the user is doing their analysis, and what sort of analytic techniques and additional data sources they might be using.

In preparation for the interviews, let me briefly review some key interviewing points and techniques to ensure interview success:

- Share the questionnaire with the interviewees before the actual interview so that they can be prepared. If you don't have an interview questionnaire, think create one.

- Allocate one hour for each interview. More time than that is typically unproductive and could indicate that your interview questions were not well thought out ahead of time. If more time is needed, schedule a separate follow-up interview.

- Leave at least 30 minutes between interviews so the interview team has time to document and assemble their notes.

- Conduct interviews in teams of 2 to 3 interviewers, designating an interview leader and a dedicated scribe. A single person should lead the interview process, with the other participants asking clarification questions only. Understand the team roles prior to the interview.

- Do not tape-record an interview. While on the surface that sounds most effective, in reality the interviewers tend to relax the interview process too much, assuming (wrongly) that what information they missed will somehow be on the tape.

Step 2: Acquire and Analyze Your Data

Next, the facilitation team should collaborate with the IT team to identify and acquire a small sample set of your data that is relevant to the targeted business initiative. This data will be used to develop a business initiative-specific "art of the possible" envisioning exercise to be used during the ideation workshop. The data scientist member of the facilitation team will be chartered to explore, enrich, and analyze the data using advanced analytics and data visualization techniques.

The analytic model is typically built on a laptop, using a combination of R (a popular, rapidly evolving, open-source analytics tool that is being widely adopted and enhanced by colleges, universities, data science organizations) and Hadoop, to accelerate model development. Building the analytic models and visualizations on a laptop eliminates the time required to acquire or provision a full analytic environment. It gives the envisioning process the flexibility needed to test other data sources that might help the analytic models. These will not be large data sets (3 to 6 GB in size), but the data needs to be relevant to the business initiative in order to develop an authentic envisioning model.

It is important to note that the purpose of building a client-specific story using analytics with the data is not to solve the business problem. Instead, it is an illustrative example designed to get the business and IT participants to start thinking about what they *might* be able to do with access to more detailed data, as well as new sources of data.

Where possible, you want to create a story with respect to the analysis; something that fuels the creative thinking process with the business users and gets them to start thinking "what if" with respect to how they might leverage the data and the analytics as part of their current responsibilities. For example, Figure 9-2 and Figure 9-3 show how a story starts to develop by using customer behavioral data to detect potential churn situations earlier in the customer engagement process. The data in Figure 9-2 can be used to leverage standard customer demographic, financial, and billing data to uncover potential churn scenarios. The data in Figure 9-3 expands on the example by adding customer behavioral data to detect potential churn situations earlier in the customer engagement process.

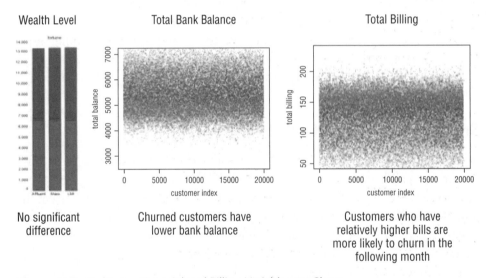

Figure 9-2: Customer Financial and Billing Variables vs. Churn

Again, the objective of creating this customer-specific envisioning exercise using customer data (which can be either customer data or mocked up customer data) is to create a *story* that helps the workshop participants to start envisioning the realm of what's possible. The customer-specific envisioning exercise helps the business stakeholders imagine what might be possible with respect to leveraging new sources of customer, product, and operational insights to improve the targeted business initiative or opportunity.

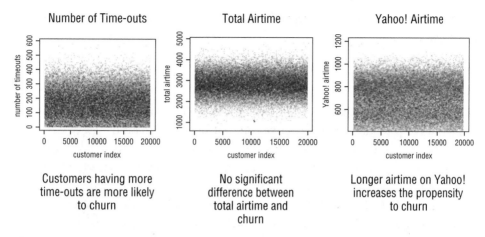

Figure 9-3: Aggregated Customer Usage Variables vs. Churn

Depending on the business initiative, the facilitation team can also expand the customer-specific envisioning exercise by incorporating data from external sources. For example, the facilitation team could capture a small subset of the organization's Facebook or twitter data to see what sorts of insights can be teased out of the social media data. Figure 9-4 shows an example analysis of customer social media data to calculate and compare customer and key competitor sentiment analysis. This type of example can fuel the creative process and help the participants to start envisioning how they might leverage social media insights as part of their targeted business initiative.

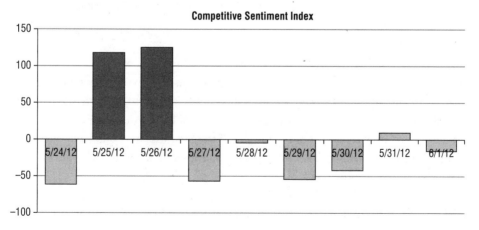

Figure 9-4: Competitive Sentiment Analysis

In this example, something happened on May 25 and 26 that warrants additional investigation. Getting the participants to start brainstorming about what might have happened before or on those days (perhaps company news, competitive activities, market news, or economic news) is a good starting point for the envisioning work that will occur in the ideation workshop.

There are also many external data sources that can be coupled with the organization's data to provide new perspectives on that same old client data. For example, www.data.gov is a valuable source of data covering a wide range of information sources which could be used to help the business users start envisioning what's possible. Figure 9-5 shows an example of integrating government-provided Consumer Price Index (CPI) data with the organization's customer sales data to ascertain if there are customer segments in which the organization's marketing spend is overcommitted or under-committed given the market segment potential.

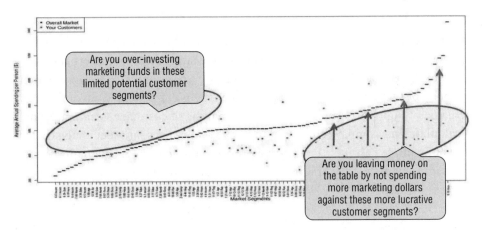

Figure 9-5: Comparison of Markets vs. Your Customers' Spending by Market Segments

Again, the objective of analyzing a small chunk of the organization's data is to personalize the linkage between the business stakeholders and the big data opportunity. You want to fuel the creative thought process to help the business stakeholders explore the realm of what might be possible if the business users had access to new customer, product, and operational insights that can be leveraged as part of their day-to-day business processes.

Step 3: Ideation Workshop: Brainstorm New Ideas

Now you're ready for the one-day ideation workshop. The goal of the ideation workshop is to employ the various business valuation techniques discussed in Chapter 7, coupled with the client-specific envisioning exercise that you just developed using the client's data, to help the business stakeholders to brainstorm how these new sources of big data (both internal and external data sources) coupled with advanced analytics can provide unique insights for use with their targeted business initiative. You'll want to inspire the business stakeholders to envision how they might leverage internal and external data sources to help them:

- Answer the business questions they need to answer in support of the targeted business initiative. You'll want to challenge them to rethink the questions they ask of the business, and to contemplate the potential business impact of answering those questions at a lower level of granularity, with new metrics (gleaned from structured and unstructured data sources, both internal and external to the organization), and across more dimensions of the business.
- Make the decisions that are necessary to support the targeted business initiative. You'll want to challenge the business users to explore more detailed, timelier, and more robust decisions enabled by access to new sources of data, coupled with advanced analytics to uncover the drivers for each of the key decisions.

The ideation workshop will cover three key envisioning steps: brainstorming, prioritization, and documentation. A sample ideation workshop agenda is shown in Table 9-1.

Table 9-1: Ideation Workshop Agenda

Minutes	Workshop Section
15	Welcome and Introductions
30	Strategic Business Initiative Discussion
	Goal: Discuss targeted business initiatives including objectives, business drivers, key performance indicators, critical success factors, and timeline
30	Share Interview Findings
	Goal: Share interview findings and some initial insights and observations
45	Data Science/Advanced Analytics Envisioning
	Goal: Stimulate creative thinking regarding how advanced analytics could energize the targeted business initiative

Continues

Table 9-1: (continued)

Minutes	Workshop Section
60	Big data Opportunities Brainstorming Goal: Use envisioning techniques to brainstorm the use cases where big data could impact targeted business initiative
60	Big data Opportunities Prioritization Goal: Use Prioritization Matrix to drive group consensus on identified use cases
30	Summarize Workshop Findings and Define Next Steps Goal: Review the list of top priority use cases and gain consensus on next steps

Brainstorming

You will start the ideation workshop by brainstorming where and how to leverage big data—new sources of customer, product, and operational data coupled with advanced and predictive analytics—to power your targeted business initiative. You will review the client-specific envisioning exercise just developed to help the business stakeholders visualize what is possible with respect to new data sources and advanced analytics tools. You will demonstrate to the business and IT stakeholders how applying advanced analytics to their internal data, coupled with third-party data as appropriate, can provide new business insights and new monetization opportunities.

You will leverage the envisioning techniques outlined in Chapter 7 (such as big data envisioning worksheet, and Michael Porter's Five Forces and Value Chain Analysis methodologies) to brainstorm the business questions, ideas, and business decisions that can supercharge the targeted business initiative. You will need to track the ideas—for example, by recording them on individual Post-it notes—in the form of business questions or statements, such as "How do I identify our most engaged customer segments?" or "I want to see what baskets of products my gold card customers typically buy."

You will want to leverage the client-specific example, as well as examples from similar and other industries, to fuel the creative thought process with respect to how other organizations and other industries are leveraging big data to drive business value. Take time to review several scenarios that will help the workshop participants envision where and how new sources of big data and advanced analytics could deliver financial and competitive value to the targeted business initiative.

The key is to challenge the group's current thinking processes and assumptions in an open, facilitated conversation. Ignite the creative processes by asking the participants to explore "what if" and "how might" thinking such as:

- *What if* I can get new insights into my customer shopping behaviors and product preferences, and *how might* that change my customer engagement opportunities?
- *What if* I had insights into my patients' current and historical lifestyles and diet patterns, and *how might* that impact my ability to diagnose their current health problems and prescribe more specific health changes?
- *What if* I knew which of my products were operating at the edges of acceptable performance, and *how might* those insights be used to improve maintenance scheduling, crew training, and inventory management?
- *What if* I knew the characteristics of my safest, most successful drivers, and *how might* those insights be used to change how I hire, train, and pay my most valuable drivers?

All of these business questions, statements, and ideas should be captured on individual Post-it notes. Capturing each of these questions, statements and ideas on a separate note is key to the grouping step that takes place next. The questions could look like the following for a client targeting a "churn reduction" business initiative:

- What customer segments are experiencing the most churn?
- Are there similarities in product usage patterns and propensities across my churning customers?
- What are the social characteristics of my highest churning customer segments?
- What are the common characteristics or usage patterns of customers who churn?
- Are there any customer segments that have experienced reduced churn?
- What marketing offers have we tested with high-probability churn customers?
- Who are our most profitable customers?
- Who are our most valuable customers?

It's not uncommon in the brainstorming session to capture 60, 80, or 120 different questions, statements, and ideas. Capture them all, and you'll sort and group them later.

Here is a list of some useful facilitation tips and techniques for managing the creative process during the facilitated, brainstorming session

- Hold the brainstorming session in a room that has an open feel to encourage open discussions and the open sharing of ideas. Explore options outside of the client's office, such as a hotel conference room or a partner's conference room. We once conducted a brainstorming session on a wind turbine farm, just to get the participants out of their comfort zone. So be creative.
- Minimize clutter by getting rid of tables and setting up chairs in a horseshoe style (avoid lecture hall or classroom set ups).
- Tape multiple flip charts on the walls around the room to capture ideas.
- Place a "parking lot" flip chart on the wall that can be used to capture discussions that may be interesting but threaten to derail the brainstorming process. It's a polite way of saying that you need to move on.
- Randomly place the Post-it notes on the multiple flip charts. Don't worry about grouping the Post-it notes as you place them on the flip charts. You'll use a grouping process in the next step in the Ideation Workshop process.
- Ensure that everyone works individually. When participants work in groups, it's not unusual that one person dominates the conversation and many good ideas from other group members never get recognized or recorded.
- Capture one idea per Post-it note. If you get a Post-it note with multiple questions, divide it into multiple Post-it notes.
- Read out loud what others have written as you place the Post-it notes on the flip charts. Reading the notes as you post them helps to fuel the creative thinking.
- Run the brainstorming session as long as anyone is still generating ideas. In fact, let silence work to your advantage by continuing to encourage folks to think of new questions, statements, and ideas.
- Give participants a heads-up that you'll stop capturing Post-it notes at 5-, 3-, and 1-minute intervals. Don't feel obligated to stick to those particular timeframes. Again, let the process run as long as it's productive.

Aggregation or Grouping

The goal of the aggregation or grouping step is to group the questions, statements, and ideas captured on the Post-it notes into common themes. Have the participants huddle around the flip charts and look for common themes amongst the Post-it notes. Move the business questions and statements into common "themes" (use cases), for example, revenue analysis, customer up-sell, customer churn, and branch performance analysis. It is not unusual to have multiple Post-it notes that are very similar because many of the business stakeholders are asking the same questions, although they may use different metrics or dimensions. For example, the Sales department might want to see sales performance by sales reps and sales territories, while the Marketing department might want to see sales performance by campaign and promotion, and the Product Development department might want to see sales performance by products and product lines. Every group is interested in sales performance, just by different dimensions of the business.

Once you have established a "theme" and have grouped the common Post-it notes together around that theme, use a marker to draw a large circle around that group of Post-its and give it a label, such as customer acquisition, customer churn, or up-sell. Keep the title or description short (three- to four-word descriptions). Later in the documentation phase, you'll flush out the themes with a more descriptive title and more details gathered from the Post-it notes associated with that theme.

Typically, the targeted business initiative will break down into multiple (6 to 12) use cases. For example, "leverage customer behavioral insights to optimize the customer lifecycle engagement processes" might break down into the following "themes" or use cases:

- Reduce churn
- Most important customer segments
- Competitive churn benchmarks
- Product usage characteristics
- Network performance trends
- Customer acquisition
- Customer profiling and segmentation
- Package audience segments
- Location-based services

The end result of the brainstorming process will be several flip charts covered with Post-it notes with the common themes or use cases grouped together (see Figure 9-6).

Figure 9-6: Using Post-it Notes for the brainstorming process

Finally, create a separate Post-it note for each identified theme or use case. These Post-it notes will be used in the prioritization exercise.

Step 4: Ideation Workshop: Prioritize Big Data Use Cases

Finally, you will guide the workshop participants through a prioritization process where each use case is judged based on its relative business value vis-à-vis its implementation feasibility. During this process, you will capture details regarding the business value drivers (for instance, why one business opportunity was valued more highly than another) and the reasons behind the feasibility determination (such as why one business opportunity is more difficult to implement than another). The end result of the prioritization process is a matrix like that shown in Figure 9-7.

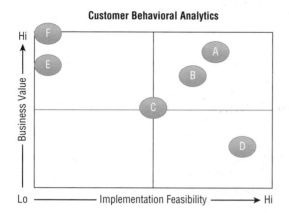

Figure 9-7: Sample prioritization results

Use Cases:

A. **Churn:** Couple smartphone app usage data with customer financial and demographic data to improve Churn Predictive Model Effectiveness

B. **Product Performance:** Drive changes to network bandwidth based upon customer's usage and customer profitability

C. **Network Optimization:** Optimize Network investments to reduce congestion based upon customers' app usage patterns

D. **Standardization:** Standardize tools, processes, analytic models, and hiring profiles across analytics teams

E. **Recommendations:** Create customer-specific product and service recommendations based upon their smartphone app usage patterns

F. **Monetization:** Leverage smartphone app usage data to drive new location-based services business opportunities

I will cover how to facilitate the prioritization process later in this chapter, as it is the key capstone activity of the ideation workshop, and turns all the prior research and brainstorming into an executable action plan.

Step 5: Document Next Steps

As the last step, you will summarize the identified and prioritized business opportunities, and recommend steps for deploying advanced analytics in support of the targeted business initiatives. You will document the results of the envisioning process which include:

■ Key interview findings as related to the targeted business initiative including key business questions, business decisions, and required data sources

- Analytic use cases that came out of the brainstorming step
- The Prioritization Matrix results including details on the placement of each use case, business value drivers, and implementation risk items
- Recommended next steps

The final stage of the vision process workshop is a presentation of the findings and recommendations, as well, as the detailed insights from the envisioning exercise, to executive management. The findings and recommendations will confirm the relevance of big data to help drive the targeted business initiative and determine next steps for implementation.

The Prioritization Process

One key challenge to a successful big data journey is gaining consensus and alignment between the business and IT stakeholders in identifying the initial big data business use cases that deliver sufficient value to the business, while possessing a high probability of success. One can find multiple business use cases where big data and advanced analytics can deliver compelling business value. However, many of these use cases have a low probability of execution success due to:

- Unavailability of timely, accurate data
- Lack of experience with new data sources like social media, mobile, logs, and telemetry data
- Limited data science or advanced analytics resources or skills
- Lack of experience with new technologies like Hadoop, MapReduce, and text mining
- Architectural and technology limitations with managing and analyzing unstructured data, and ingesting and analyzing real-time data feeds
- Weak working relationship between the business and IT teams
- Lack of management fortitude and support

I have found one tool for driving business and IT collaboration and agreement around identifying the right initial use cases for your big data journey—those with sufficient business value and a high probability of success. This tool is the *Prioritization Matrix*. Let me share how the Prioritization Matrix works to not only prioritize the initial big data use cases, but how to use it to foster an atmosphere of collaboration between the business and IT stakeholders.

The prioritization process is the single most important step in the envisioning process. While I expect that most readers would think the brainstorming process is the most important, the truth is that many use cases are probably already known ahead of the brainstorming session. The brainstorming session is useful in validating and expanding on those known use cases and helping to fuel the identification of additional use cases.

But if you cannot gain group consensus on the right use cases on which to start your big data initiative, then the big data initiative has a greatly diminished chance of success. To be successful, the big data initiative needs the initial support *and on-going leadership* of both business and IT stakeholders in order to drive the potential business transformation. Let's start the prioritization process lesson by first understanding the mechanics of the Prioritization Matrix.

The Prioritization Matrix is a 2×2 grid that facilitates the interactive process and debate between the business and IT stakeholders to determine where on the matrix to place each use case in relation to the other use cases. The use cases are placed on the matrix based on:

- **Business value**: the vertical axis of the matrix. The business stakeholders are typically responsible for the relative positioning of each business use case on the Business Value axis. The Business Value axis reads from low business value at the bottom to high business value at the top as shown in Figure 9-8.
- **Implementation feasibility**: the probability of a successful implementation considering availability, granularity and timeliness of data, skills, tools, organizational readiness, and needed experience. Implementation feasibility is the horizontal axis of the matrix. The IT stakeholders are typically responsible for the relative positioning of each business use case on the Implementation Feasibility axis. The Implementation Feasibility axis reads from low implementation feasibility on the left (higher probability of failure) to high implementation feasibility on the right (higher probability of success).

As a reminder, you are not looking for the exact valuation of each use case from a Business Value perspective. Instead, you want to know the relative business value of each use case and some level of justification from the business stakeholders as to the reasoning behind the placement of the use case.

Figure 9-8: The Prioritization Matrix

The Prioritization Matrix Process

Focusing the Prioritization Matrix process on a key business initiative—such as reducing churn, increasing same store sales, minimizing financial risk, optimizing market spend, or reducing hospital readmissions—is critical as it provides the foundation upon which the business value and implementation feasibility discussion can occur.

The Prioritization Matrix process starts by placing each use case identified in the brainstorming and aggregation stages on a Post-it note (one use case per Post-it). The group, which must include both business and IT stakeholders, decides the placement of each use case on the Prioritization Matrix by weighing business value and implementation feasibility, vis-à-vis the relative placement of the other use cases on the matrix.

The business stakeholders are responsible for the relative positioning of each business case on the Business Value axis, while the IT stakeholders are primarily responsible for the relative positioning of each business case on the Implementation Feasibility axis (considering data, technology, skills, and organizational readiness).

The heart of the prioritization process is the discussion that ensues about the relative placement of each of the use cases (see Figure 9-10), such as:

- Why is use case [B] more or less valuable than use case [A]? What are the specific business drivers or variables that make use case [B] more or less valuable than use case [A]? (See Figure 9-9.)
- Why is use case [B] less or more feasible from an implementation perspective than use case [A]? What are the specific implementation risks that make use case [B] less or more feasible than use case [A]?

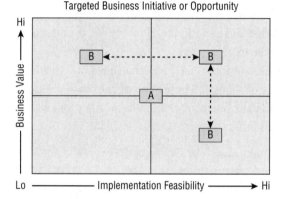

Figure 9-9: Prioritization process drives group alignment

It is critical to the prioritization process to capture the reasons for the relative positioning of each use case, in order to identify the critical business value drivers and potential implementation risks.

Prioritization Matrix Traps

One of the keys to affectively using the Prioritization Matrix is to understand the potential discussion traps and to guide the workshop participants around those traps. In particular, you want to avoid use cases that fall into the following matrix zones (see Figure 9-10):

- "Zone of Mismanaged Expectations" are those use cases with huge business value but little chance of successful execution (for example, solve world hunger). It is not uncommon for a senior executive to have a pet project that is grand in vision and scale. The Prioritization Matrix will highlight the specific reasons why that might be a poor use case against which to start your big data journey. The Prioritization Matrix process will also highlight what steps need to be taken to move the use case into a more highly feasible situation.

■ "Zone of User Disillusionment" are those use cases which are easy to execute but provide little business value. These types of use cases tend to be technological science experiments, where the IT group has developed some skills in a new technology or has gained access to some new data sources and are desperately trying to find a use case against which to apply their new capabilities. Don't go there. While there is always room within IT for experiments in order to develop more knowledge and experience, don't make your business stakeholders guinea pigs in those experiments.

■ "Zone of Career-limiting Moves" are those use cases that have little business value and have a low probability of success. These sorts of use cases should be self-evident and no one on either the business or IT sides of the room should want to target one of these use cases.

Figure 9-10: Prioritization Matrix traps

Use cases that fall into one of these zones should be avoided because they either don't provide enough business value to be meaningful to the business stakeholders, or are too risky to IT from an implementation perspective.

It is important to note that understanding where each use case falls, and the open discussion between the business and IT stakeholders about why each use case is positioned where it is, is key to understanding the implementation and business risks and avoiding surprises once the project is implemented—Eyes wide open!

Finally, the end result of the Prioritization Matrix process will look something like that shown in Figure 9-11. All the use cases have been placed on the Prioritization Matrix and justification for both the business value and implementation feasibility discussed and agreed upon. The use cases in the upper-right quadrant of Figure 9-11 end up being the "low-hanging fruit" for your initial big data engagement.

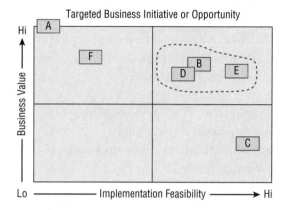

Figure 9-11: Prioritization Matrix end result

The prioritization matrix is a marvelous tool for facilitating a conversation between the business and IT stakeholders about where and how to start the big data journey. It provides a framework for identifying the relative business value of each business use case (with respect to the targeted business initiative) and for identifying and understanding the implementation risks. Out of this prioritization process, both the business and IT stakeholders should know what use cases they are targeting and the potential business value of each use case. Participants also have their eyes wide open to the implementation risks that the project needs to avoid or manage.

Using User Experience Mockups to Fuel the Envisioning Process

Developing simple user experience mockups is a powerful way to help the business users "envision the realm of what's possible." Organizations can combine big data concepts with user experience mockups to help break out of their current mental boxes—to think differently—and identify new ways that big data can power the organization's value creation processes. The new customer, product, and operational insights gathered from these mockups can also help identify new revenue or monetization opportunities. Let's review a few examples of how a simple mockup can help drive the envisioning process.

The following example takes an organization's website or mobile apps and poses some challenging questions about how the organization could improve the website or app to drive a more engaging customer experience. The mockup shows a credit union that released a smartphone app to support their new "MyBranch" customer engagement initiative (see Figure 9-12). (Note: All of the information used to create this mockup was retrieved from the credit union's public-facing website.) The new smartphone app supports the following customer transactions:

- View current and available balances across all the customers' accounts
- Transfer funds between accounts or make loan payments
- View transaction history and access details on specific transactions
- Electronically pay bills anywhere and anytime
- Get directions to the nearest branch or ATM
- Set alerts on account balances, debit card transactions, and withdrawals

Figure 9-12: Mobile app functionality mockup

These customer transactions are a ripe source of customer insights and product preferences that can be mined to provide a more compelling and relevant user experience. That same user experience can also yield new customer and product insights that can be converted into new monetization opportunities such as new services and products. With this mockup in hand, the business users can now be taken through a series of envisioning exercises to explore and brainstorm the following types of questions (see Figure 9-13):

- What are the usage patterns of my most valuable customers?
- What are the usage patterns that indicate someone may be churning?
- How do we leverage personalized insights and previous activities to improve the customer experience?
- How can we provide additional features, such as social media, to capture more information about our customers' interests, passions, associations, and affiliations?
- How can we leverage these insights, coupled with the GPS features of our smartphone apps, to offer location-based customer services?
- How can we leverage recommendations to enhance the customer experience?
- How can we capture lifestyle goals, such as saving to buy a home or new car?
- Are there instrumentation opportunities we can use to gain insights into our customers' behaviors, preferences, and interests?
- Are their combinations of features that we can re-engineer to improve the customer experience?

I hope you can realize how powerful even simple mockups can be in helping the vision workshop business and IT stakeholders identify how big data can power an improved customer experience and uncover new monetization opportunities. A simple customer experience mockup can bring to life the potential of big data to:

- Identify additional opportunities to capture customer usage and product preference data through additional instrumentation of the website and smartphone apps
- Leverage advanced analytics to uncover customer-specific insights, recommendations, and benchmarks to power a more relevant and compelling user experience

■ Leverage experimentation techniques to tease out more customer and product insights by presenting different recommendations to see which audiences respond to which offers and recommendations

The mockup in Figure 9-13 is a little more advanced and explores how a cellular provider could leverage their subscribers' app usage data to improve the subscriber's user experience—make the experience more relevant and actionable—in order to improve customer engagement processes and uncover new monetization opportunities.

This example evaluates how a cellular phone company could leverage a subscriber's app usage data, and the app usage behaviors of similar customers, to develop personalized e-mail recommendations that might be beneficial to that subscriber. In the process, the cellular provider will learn more about their subscribers' preferences— what they like and what they don't like—that can yield even more subscriber and product insights. This is a counter-example to the "unintelligent" user experience presented in Chapter 8.

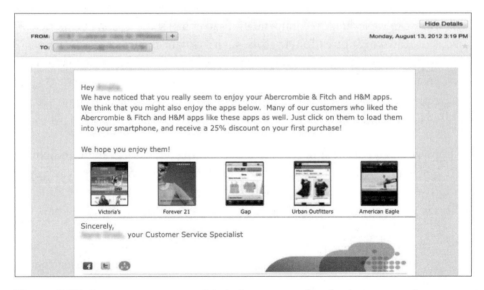

Figure 9-13: Leverage apps usage data to improve a subscriber's user experience

There are numerous "what if" questions that could fuel the brainstorming process for this mockup, such as:

■ What if we could leverage our subscribers' app usage patterns to recommend apps that move the user into a more profitable, high-retention usage category (for example, from "Moderate Female Teenage Browser" to "Female Teenage Shopaholic")?

- What if we could score the customers' app usage patterns to identify and act on potential churn situations more quickly?
- What if we could integrate app performance data across our subscriber base to recommend apps that provide a superior customer experience and help create more loyalty to the cellular provider?
- What if we could aggregate subscriber app usage insights across the entire network to create new monetization opportunities, such as app developer referral fees and co-marketing fees?
- What if we could integrate customers' app usage insights with real-time GPS location information to offer personalized location-based services?

Creating mockups is an effective technique for fueling the creative thinking process during the ideation workshop. Don't be concerned about the professional level of mockup (my mockups look like I drew them with a crayon). It's more important that the mockups challenge the current conventional thinking of the business stakeholders. The mockups can push the business stakeholders out of their current thinking ruts to contemplate the realm of what might be possible by leveraging all their customer and product insights to optimize existing customer engagement processes and uncover new monetization opportunities.

Summary

This chapter reviewed in detail the vision workshop or envisioning process. I described each of the five steps in the vision workshop methodology and provided details on each step using real-world examples.

You spent quite a bit of time on the data preparation and analysis work required to transform business initiative-specific data into an envisioning exercise that can be used as part of the ideation workshop. This is an important part of the vision workshop methodology because it helps the envisioning process *come to life* for the workshop participants. I provided several examples of creating customer-specific envisioning exercises.

You learned about the brainstorming and aggregation process of the ideation workshop. You also reviewed how to use the Michael Porter value creation processes—Value Chain and Five Forces Analysis—as well as the business initiative-specific envisioning exercise to tease out new business opportunities as part of the envisioning process.

You also learned how to use the Prioritization Matrix to drive agreement between the business and IT stakeholders around the right use cases on which to start the big data journey.

The chapter concluded with a discussion on how to leverage user experience mockups in the ideation workshop to further enhance the brainstorming process. I provided a couple of sample mockups and demonstrated how to use those mockups to drive the "what if" creative thinking process.

10 Solution Engineering

You are now ready to tie all the previous exercises and envisioning work into a solution. But what is meant by a "solution," and what special skills and processes are necessary to architect a solution?

The trouble with big data is that there is no one shiny technical solution. You can't just install Hadoop, predictive analytics, or a data appliance and assume it will provide a big data solution. The data industry has struggled with this dilemma before, as data warehousing and business intelligence technologies sought relevance within organizations over the past 10 to 15 years. To be successful with big data and advanced analytics—like its brethren data warehousing and business intelligence before it—requires a new engineering skill, something called *solution engineering*.

There's engineering for many disciplines—system engineering, electrical engineering, mechanical engineering—so why not solution engineering? Solution engineering would be defined as:

> *A process for identifying and breaking down an organization's key business initiatives into its business enabling capabilities and supporting technology components in order to support an organization's decision-making and data monetization efforts.*

Let's take a look at the steps of the solution engineering process.

NOTE Some key materials and graphics have been duplicated from previous chapters in order to make this a stand-alone chapter.

The Solution Engineering Process

Surprisingly, the solution engineering process is similar to working with LEGO bricks. The most successful LEGO projects are those that have an end in mind—a thoroughly defined, well-scoped solution. Do I want to build the pirate ship, the castle, or the space station? With LEGO bricks, I can build all three, plus many,

many more. However, each solution requires a different set of bricks in different configurations and a different set of instructions. Much like LEGO bricks, it is critical to your big data business success to identify up-front what solution your organization is trying to build, and then to assemble and integrate the right data and technology capabilities with the right instructions or roadmap to deliver a successful solution.

In this section I outline a 6-step solution engineering process for identifying, architecting, and developing a business solution (see Figure 10-1). This six-step solution engineering process encompasses the following:

1. Understand how the organization makes money
2. Identify your organization's key business initiatives
3. Brainstorm big data business impact
4. Break down the business initiative into use cases
5. Prove out the use case
6. Design and implement the big data solution

This process requires an up-front investment of time and creative thinking to grasp how your organization makes money. This means that you need to invest the time to identify your organization's *strategic nouns*; that is, those strategic business entities—like customers, stores, employees, and products—around which your organization builds differentiated business processes (e.g., acquisition, retention, optimization, management). You need to understand the role that these strategic nouns play in your organization's value creation processes. You need to identify the organization's key business initiatives and understand the desired impact of these initiatives on the organization's strategic nouns. This knowledge and information will guide and focus your solution engineering efforts. These are all activities for which approaches and methodologies were provided in Chapter 7.

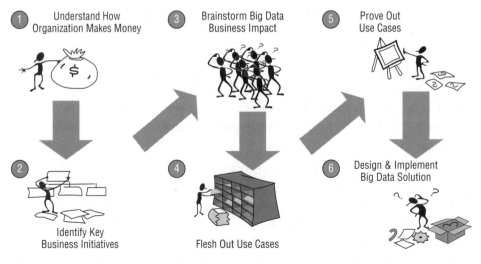

Figure 10-1 Solution engineering process

Step 1: Understand How the Organization Makes Money

Pretend that you are the general manager of the organization. Take the time to contemplate how the organization can make more money. For example, what can the organization do to increase revenues, decrease costs, reduce risks, or increase compliance?

There are many levers an organization can pull in order to make more money. Increasing revenue, for example, can include initiatives such as increasing the number of premium or gold card customers, increasing store or site traffic, reducing customer churn, increasing revenue per shopping occurrence, increasing private label sales as a percentage of market basket, increasing cross-sell/upsell effectiveness, and optimizing promotional effectiveness (see Figure 10-2). Reducing costs can include reducing inventory and supply chains costs, reducing fraud and shrinkage, improving marketing spend effectiveness, consolidating suppliers, improving on-time pickups and deliveries, optimizing merchandise markdowns, and improving asset utilization and turns.

Sales & Marketing	**Operations**	**Finance**
• Acquire more customers	• Optimize network performance	• Rationalize products
• Retain existing customers	• Predict maintenance problems	• Close unprofitable channels
• Cross-sell/up-sell	• Eliminate shrinkage	• Increase inventory turns
• Increase market basket	• Predict utilization/capacity	• Increase asset utilization
• Increase store traffic	• Increase fill-rates	• Reduce DSO
• Optimize pricing and yield	• Reduce out-of-stocks	• Reduce SG&A
• Increase conversion rate	• Consolidate suppliers	• Reduce T&E
• Improve ad effectiveness		• Reduce fraud and waste

Figure 10-2: High potential big data business opportunity

Next, spend the time to identify and understand your organization's strategic nouns, and ascertain how those nouns drive the moneymaking capabilities of the organization. For example, if you're in the airline industry, hubs are a very important noun used in your business, and any way that you can increase the number of flights per hub (such as decreasing airplane turnaround times or improving terminal and ramp efficiencies) means more flights per day, which equals more money. If you're in the movie theater business, then concessions is a very important noun and any way you can increase the concession market baskets of theater guests (for example, buying a soda with the popcorn or buying the large water bottle versus the small water bottle) equals more money.

Finally, invest time actually using your organization's products or services. Experience first-hand how your organization's product or products work. Become a customer, become familiar with the user experience and understand the product's value propositions to its customers and partners. This will help you identify and understand the organization's key moneymaking and value creation activities that could be impacted by big data.

With these observations in hand, you are now prepared to put pen to paper and start to envision ideas on where new sources of customer, product, and operations insights could power your organization's ability to make more money. For example, if your organization is in the Business-to-Consumer (B2C) market, you can easily imagine how the organization could leverage both internal customer engagement data (such as e-mail, consumer comments, service logs, or physician notes) as well as external customer engagement data (such as social media postings, service ratings like Yelp, or blogs) to uncover insights that can help to optimize the customer engagement processes (for instance, profiling, segmentation, targeting, acquisition, activation, maturation, retention, and advocacy) in order to create more "profitable" customers (see Figure 10-3).

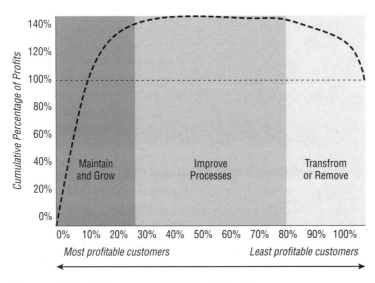

Figure 10-3: Customer profitability distribution

Source: R. S. Kaplan and S. Anderson, "Time-driven Activity-based Costing," *Harvard Business Review* (November 2004)

As we discussed in Chapter 8, across most industries:

- 0 to 25% of customers drive greater than 100% of profits
- 50 to 60% deliver no profits
- 10 to 25% deliver negative profits

Consequently, the solution engineering challenge in B2C industries is to determine how to leverage big data analytics to:

1. Move customers "up" the profitability curve (e.g., cross-selling them additional products, up-selling them more profitable products and services, replacing branded products with private label products to increase market basket profitability)
2. Service unprofitable customers in a more cost-effective manner (e.g., via the web, using self-service, through partners)

Step 2: Identify Your Organization's Key Business Initiatives

The next step is to do some primary research to understand your organization's key business initiatives. This includes reading the annual report, listening to analyst calls, and searching for recent executive management speeches and presentations. If possible, interview senior business management to understand their top business initiatives and opportunities, as well as their perceptions of the key challenges that might prevent the organization from successfully executing against their top business opportunities. (I will provide suggestions and examples on how to read an organization's annual report or public statements to uncover big data business opportunities later in this chapter.)

For each identified business initiative or opportunity, capture key information such as:

- Business stakeholders and their roles, responsibilities, and expectations
- Key performance indicators and the metrics against which success of the business initiative will be measured
- Timeframe for delivery
- Critical success factors
- Desired outcomes
- Key tasks

NOTE Review Chapter 6 on using the big data strategy document to break down your organization's business strategy into its key business initiatives, desired outcomes, and critical success factors.

Step 3: Brainstorm Big Data Business Impact

The next step in the solution engineering process is to brainstorm how big data and advanced analytics can impact the targeted business initiative. As discussed in Chapter 7, there are four ways (the four "Big Data Business Drivers"; see Table 10-1) that big data and advanced analytics can power an organization's key business initiatives:

1. Mine the more detailed transactional (dark) data at the lowest level of trans-action granularity, which enables more granular and detailed decisions. For example, analyze the detailed transactional data, such as customer loyalty transactions, to enable more granular decision making and uncover new data monetization opportunities at the individual customer, seasonal/holiday, and location/geography levels.

2. Integrate new unstructured data sources to enable more robust and complete decisions. This includes internal unstructured data sources such as consumer comments, call center notes, e-mail, physician notes, and service bay logs, as well as external unstructured data sources such as social media posts, blogs, mobile/smartphone apps, and third-party or public data sources. I would also include sensor-generated data, such as smart grids, connected cars, and smart appliances, in this category. These new diverse data sources provide new variables, metrics, and dimensions that can be integrated into analytic models to yield actionable and material business insights and recommendations.

3. Provide real-time/low-latency data access where you reduce the time delay between when the data event occurs and the analysis of that data event, which enables more frequent and timely decisions and data monetization. This could include the creation of on-demand customer segments (based on the results of some major event like the Super Bowl) as well as real-time location-based insights from smartphones and mobile apps.

4. Integrate predictive analytics into your key business processes to provide new opportunities to uncover causality (cause and effect) buried in the data. Predictive analytics enable a different mindset with your business stakehold-ers, encouraging them to use new verbs—like optimize, predict, recommend, score, and forecast—as they explore new data monetization opportunities.

Table 10-1: Big Data Business Value Drivers

Big Data Business Drivers	Data Monetization Impacts
Transactional (dark) Data: More Detailed Transactional Data (e.g., POS, CDR, RFID, Credit Card)	Enable more granular, more detailed decisions (localization, seasonality, multi-dimensionality)
Unstructured Data: Diverse Internal (e-mail, consumer comments) and External (social media, mobile) Data	Enable more complete and more accurate decisions (new metrics, dimensions, and dimensional attributes)
Data Velocity: Low-latency ("Real-time") Data Access	Enable more frequent, more timely decisions (hourly versus weekly; on-demand analytic model updates)
Predictive Analytics: Causality, Predictors, Instrumentation, Experimentation	More actionable, predictive decisions (Optimize, Recommend, Predict, Score, Forecast)

Later in this chapter I will provide some examples across different industries of how to leverage these four big data business drivers to create business solutions.

Step 4: Break Down the Business Initiative Into Use Cases

The next step is to conduct a series of interviews and ideation/envisioning workshops to brainstorm, identify, define, aggregate, and prioritize the use cases necessary to support the targeted business initiative. As discussed in the Vision Workshop section of Chapter 9, you want to capture the following information for each identified use case:

- Targeted personas and stakeholders, including their roles, responsibilities, and expectations
- Business questions the business stakeholders are trying to answer, or could be trying to answer if they had access to more detailed and diverse data sources

- Business decisions the business stakeholders are trying to make, and the supporting decision processes including timing, decision flow/process, and downstream stakeholders
- Key performance indicators and key metrics against which business success will be measured
- Data requirements including sources, availability, access methods, update frequency, granularity, dimensionality, and hierarchies
- Identify analytic algorithms and modeling requirements such as prediction, forecasting, optimization, and recommendations
- Capture user experience requirements, which should couple closely with the user's decision-making process

This is great time to deploy the prioritization matrix methodology to use group dynamics to prioritize the different business use cases, and build IT and business consensus and support to move forward on the top use cases.

NOTE Step 3 and step 4 are great opportunities to use the previously discussed ideation workshop process described in Chapter 9 to brainstorm new ideas, aggregate the ideas into business relevant use cases, and prioritize the use cases based upon a weighting of business value and implementation feasibility.

Step 5: Prove Out the Use Case

Now is the time to deploy data and technology to validate the analytic feasibility of the solution. This is a good time to introduce a Proof of Value analytic lab to prove out the business case (financial model, ROI and analytic lift) using the full depth of available data and full breadth of available technology capabilities. You have a detailed definition of the desired solution including key decisions, business questions, key performance indicators, and all the other solution details captured in step 4. At this point, you should also have a solid understanding of the required data (such as data sources, key metrics, levels of granularity, frequency of access, dimensionality, and others) and the necessary technology and analytic capabilities to build out the Proof of Value. This Proof of Value analytic lab process should include:

- Gathering required data from both internal and external data sources, and integrate the data into a single data platform. You want the detailed data, not the aggregated data, because you're going to want to mine the detailed data to uncover the material, significant and actionable nuances buried in the data. You should also explore the use of third-party data, some of it publicly available from sources like `www.data.gov`, to help broaden the quality of the analytics. This is also a great time to bring in social media data, especially if you are dealing with a customer-centric use case.

- Defining and executing data transformation processes necessary to cleanse, align, and prepare the data for analysis. This most likely will include several data enrichment processes in order to create new composite metrics—such as frequency (how often an event occurs), recency (how recently the event occurred), and sequencing (in what sequence did the events occur)—that may be better predictors of business performance.

- Defining the analytic test plan including the test hypotheses, test cases, and measurement criteria.

- Developing and fine-tuning analytic models against defined key performance indicators and critical success factors. The data scientists involved in this step will likely continue to explore new data sources and new data transformation techniques that may help improve the reliability and predictability of the analytic models.

- Defining user experience requirements—in particular, understanding the downstream constituents of the analytic results and how the analytic results will need to be consumed by those constituents.

- Developing mockups and/or wireframes that help the business stakeholders understand how the resulting analytic results and models will be integrated into their daily business processes.

The goal of the Proof of Value analytic lab is to prove out the business case (including financial return or ROI, business user requirements, and critical success criteria), as well as to create and validate the underlying data models and analytic models that will provide the analytic lift. You want to validate that the integration of massive amounts of detailed structured and unstructured data coupled with advanced analytics can result in a more predictive, real-time analytic model that can deliver material meaningful and actionable insights and recommendations for the targeted business solution.

Step 6: Design and Implement the Big Data Solution

Based on the success of the Proof of Value analytic lab process, it's now time to start defining and building the detailed data models, analytic models, technology architectures, and production roadmap for integrating the analytic models and insights into the key operational and management systems. The implementation plan and roadmap will need to address the following:

- **Data sources and data access requirements**: This should include a detailed plan and roadmap for prioritizing what data to capture and where to store that data (both from a data access, as well as an analysis perspective). This plan will need to address both structured and unstructured data. It also needs to address external data sources, which means that the data plan will need to be updated every 4 to 6 months to accommodate the many new data sources that are becoming available.

- **Instrumentation strategy**: It is likely that additional data about your customers, products, and operations will need to be captured, mainly out of the existing business processes. The instrumentation strategy will need to cover how additional tags, cookies, and other instrumentation techniques can be used to capture additional transactional data.

- **Real-time data access and analysis requirements**: Certain use cases are going to require real-time (or low-latency) data access, analysis, and decision making as data is flowing through the business. These real-time requirements must be addressed across your entire technology and architectural stack including your Extract, Transform, and Load (ETL) and Extract, Load, and Transform (ELT) algorithms, data transformation and enrichment processes, in-memory computing, complex event processing, data platform, analytic models, and user experience.

- **Data management capabilities:** The big data industry has gained lots of experience and has developed many excellent tools and methodologies for helping organizations in the data management space (such as, master data management, data quality, and data governance). However, organizations also need to address when the data quality is good enough given the types of decisions and business processes that are being supported. Organizations need to carefully think through this question so that time is not wasted trying to make imperfect data perfect, especially when the decisions and the business processes that the data will support do not need perfection (for example, ad serving, fraud detection, location-based marketing, and markdown management). This part of the solution requires understanding and answering the "When is 90-percent accurate data good enough?" question.

- **Data modeling capabilities:** Data modeling requirements need to encompass all the traditional data warehousing architectural approaches—operational data store, data staging area, data marts, enterprise data warehouse—plus many of the new data platform and data federation tools and techniques that are available. The data modeling plan will need to consider data schema design and the role of NoSQL databases (where NoSQL stands for "Not Only SQL"), Hadoop and the Hadoop Distributed File System (HDFS).

- **Business intelligence:** Most organizations have an existing business intelligence or Business Performance Monitoring (BPM) environment in place that addresses key performance indicators, reporting, alerts, and dashboard requirements. This is the time to determine how to enhance that investment with new big data capabilities such as unstructured data, real-time data feeds, and predictive analytics. As discussed in the Business Model Maturity index section of Chapter 1, organizations have already invested a considerable amount of time, money, and people resources to build a BI environment around many of their critical internal business processes. Now is the time to develop a plan for how best to leverage and expand on those BI investments.

- **Advanced analytic capabilities (statistical analysis, predictive modeling, and data mining):** This is the realm of the data science organization and much has already been discussed about the importance of creating an environment where the data science team is free to do their jobs. (I'll also discuss some high-level architectural components of an analytic sandbox in the next chapter.) Organizations should also start to develop an experimentation strategy that calls out the areas of the business where experimentation is going to be used to gain additional insights about customers, products, and operations.

- **User experience requirements:** The user experience plan needs to include the wireframe and mockup processes to ensure an understanding of how the analytic results and models will manifest themselves into the business users' daily operations and the management reports and dashboards. Use this opportunity to understand the user experience requirements of your internal users, external customers, and business partners, and to capture how analytic insights will be integrated into those user environments.

Solution Engineering Tomorrow's Business Solutions

While solution engineering might not be tomorrow's sexy job, it will become more and more important as the amount and variety of data continue to evolve, technology capabilities continue to expand (fueled by both venture capitalists and the explosive growth of the open source movement), and as mobile devices and smaller form-factor mobile apps redefine the user experience. As the data and technology sands are shifting under your feet, it will become even more important that you are focused on delivering business solutions that have a high return on investment and a short payback period.

So how do you leverage these big data business drivers to explore or envision how big data and advanced analytics can help you define and deliver solutions that drive your key business initiatives? Let's walk through some examples.

Customer Behavioral Analytics Example

The big data opportunity in customer behavioral analytics is to combine your detailed customer transactions (such as sales, returns, consumer comments, and web clicks) with new social media and mobile data. The goal of combining these is to uncover new customer insights that can optimize your customer engagement lifecycle processes, such as profiling, targeting, segmenting, acquisition, activation, cross-sell/up-sell, retention, and advocacy. These same customer and product insights can ultimately lead to personalized marketing, especially when coupled with the real-time customer activity and location data that can be obtained via mobile apps. To gain new insights about your customers' behaviors, your organization could implement the following solutions:

- Integrate all of your detailed customer engagement transactions, such as sales history, returns, payment history, customer loyalty, call center notes, consumer comments, e-mail conversations, and web clicks into a single or virtual data repository.
- Use advanced analytics to analyze the detailed customer engagement transactions to model and score your most valuable customers and customer segments, create more granular behavioral categories, and use these behavioral categories and customer scores to refine your target customer profiles and customer segmentation strategies.
- Integrate and cleanse all of your prospect data—such as name, company, and contact information—gathered via lead generation events and third-party market sources.
- Augment the customer and prospect data with third-party data, from vendors such as Acxiom, Experian, BlueKai, and nPario, with customer demographic information, such as age, sex, education level, income level, and household information.
- Capture and aggregate relevant social media data about your products, services, and company from sites such as Facebook, Twitter, LinkedIn, Yelp, Pinterest, and others.

- Search, monitor, and capture relevant product and company comments from product and company advocates and dissenters located on blog sites such as WordPress, Blogger, and Tumblr.
- Use text analytics and/or Hadoop/MapReduce to mine the social media and blog data to uncover new insights about your customers' interests, passions, affiliations, and associations that can be used to refine your target customer profiles and customer segmentation models.
- Leverage mobile app capabilities to uncover real-time insights about your customers' locations, purchase behaviors, and propensities in order to drive real-time location-based promotions, offers, and communications.

Predictive Maintenance Example

Maybe the most significant opportunity for business-to-business (B2B) companies in the big data space is the opportunity to provide predictive maintenance services to their business (and possibly consumer) markets. Big data analytics can leverage sensor-generated data from appliances, equipment, implements, and machinery to analyze, score, and predict the maintenance requirements in real-time. Any industry that operates machinery—such as automobiles, airplanes, trains, farming machinery, construction equipment, appliances, energy equipment, turbines, servers, business equipment—can benefit from predictive maintenance that is enabled by the combination of sensor-generated data coupled with real-time analytics. To gain new predictive maintenance insights, organizations could architect the following solution:

- Capture raw unstructured appliance, equipment, implement, and machinery sensor-generated logs and error codes in real-time *as-is* (with no data preprocessing required, and no predefined data schemas) into Hadoop and HDFS.
- Use advanced analytics against your historical performance data to build predictive models of what constitutes "normal" appliance, equipment, and machinery performance at the individual unit and component levels. Six Sigma techniques, such as control charts, can be very useful to identify unusual product performance. Plus, Six Sigma is a methodology that is typically well understood within manufacturing industries.
- Leverage advanced data enrichment techniques, such as frequency, recency, and sequencing metrics to identify combinations of events or event thresholds that may be indicative of maintenance needs. Think about creating a "basket"

of activities that can be mined using market basket or association analytic modeling algorithms.

- Integrate external dynamic data sources such as weather (temperature, rainfall, snow, ice, humidity, and wind), traffic, and economic data sources, to identify new variables that can enhance the predictive models. For example, ascertain what impact humidity might have on the performance of your wind turbines or the impact rain and snow have on the on-time performance of your trains.

- Leverage a real-time analytics environment to monitor real-time streaming sensor data, to compare the feeds in real-time to your performance models and control charts, and then flag, score, and rank any potential performance problems.

- Send out automated alerts to concerned parties (such as technicians or consumers) including recommended maintenance information (like location, projected replacement parts, projected maintenance crew skills, and maintenance best practices documentation), and create optimized service schedules, calendars, and crew scheduling.

- Capture product or component wear data from replaced parts at the time of maintenance to continuously refine predictive maintenance models at the individual appliance/machinery and component levels.

- Aggregate and analyze wear data in order to create, package, and sell performance insights back to appliance, machinery, product, and component manufacturers.

Marketing Effectiveness Example

Every company spends money on marketing and increasingly portions of that spend are being spent in highly measurable digital media channels. Quantifying the effectiveness of marketing spend across the online—as well as offline channels such as TV, print, and radio—is a difficult challenge. Organizations that can more accurately quantify and attribute credit to the marketing channels and marketing treatments that are driving business and sales performance are better positioned to optimize marketing spend. To better measure marketing effectiveness, organizations could craft the following solution:

- Aggregate all marketing spend, at the lowest level of detail, across all digital channels (impressions, display, search, social, and mobile) as well as offline channels (TV, print, and radio).

- Integrate all sales activities and transactions (calls, bids, proposals, and sales losses and wins) with online conversion events, and associate these activities back to the different marketing activities and spend.

- For digital data, capture and aggregate into a market basket the impressions, displays, key word searches, social media post, web clicks, mouse overs, and associated conversion events at the individual user level (cookie-level detail).

- Calculate advanced composite metrics associated with marketing treatment frequency, recency, and sequencing in order to quantify the effectiveness of the different marketing treatments (attribution analysis).

- Augment campaign data with external data such as weather, seasonality, local economic, local events, and other similar data to improve campaign modeling and predictive effectiveness.

- Benchmark current campaign performance against previous and similar ("like") campaigns to identify and quantify previous campaign performance drivers.

- Leverage prospect data captured via third-party direct marketing campaigns to build out your prospective database against which you will run your direct marketing campaigns.

- Acquire new sources of customer digital insights from DMP vendors like BlueKai and nPario.

- Develop an experimentation strategy to test the effectiveness of different marketing treatments, messaging, and channels.

- Analyze social media data to capture consumer interests, passions, affiliations, and associations that can improve profiling, segmentation, and targeting effectiveness.

- Capture real-time social media feeds to analyze, monitor, and act on campaign and product sentiment trends in real-time.

- Use the insights from the marketing performance analytics and insights to drive both pre-campaign media mix allocation recommendations (such as, how to allocate marketing spend between different marketing channels like TV, print, online, display, keywords, and others) and in-flight campaign performance recommendations (such as, how to reallocate digital media spend between ad networks, keywords, target audiences, and similar items).

Fraud Reduction Example

Big data provides new and innovative technologies to identify potentially fraudulent activities in real-time. New data sources (such as social media and detailed web and mobile activities) and new big data innovations (like real-time analytics) are enabling organizations to move beyond the traditional static fraud models to create dynamic, self-learning fraud models that flag behavioral and transactional activities as they are occurring, as well as combinations of activities, that are potentially fraudulent. Here is an example of a big data fraud detection solution:

- Deploy a real-time data platform that can capture and manage a high volume of real-time data feeds (such as purchases, authorizations, and returns) from multiple internal and external data sources.
- Use in-database analytics to accelerate the development and refinement of fraud prediction models based on historical transactions.
- Use predictive analytics to analyze real-time transactions to score unusual transactions, behaviors, and tendencies across thousands of dimensions and dimensional combinations, and compare those scores to historical norms to flag potential fraud situations.
- Employ advanced data enrichment techniques—such as frequency, recency, and sequencing of activities and transactions—to create more advanced profiles of potentially fraudulent activities, behaviors, and propensities.
- Integrate mobile data with location-based analytics to dynamically identify and monitor locations, businesses, and other places that have a higher than normal propensity for potentially fraudulent behaviors (for example, gas stations, discount retailers, and convenience stores).
- Integrate real-time fraud detection models into operational systems (such as point-of-sale systems, call centers, and consumer messaging systems) to enable real-time challenging of specific transactions and groupings of transactions, with the goal of challenging those transactions while they are still in process.
- Leverage social media data to identify networks or associations of potential fraud cohorts.

Network Optimization Example

Whether you operate a network of devices (servers, ATM, switching stations, or wind turbines) or outlets (stores, sites, or branches), there are invaluable sources of new customer and product data that can be leveraged to ensure you have the "right nodes in the right locations at the right time" to provide an "exhilarating" customer experience. Over and undercapacity are always key challenges to networks, and those capacity requirements and needs can change rapidly based on customer and product behaviors and tendencies. To optimize your network operations, here is what a network optimization solution might include:

- Aggregate your network "node" data at the lowest level of detail (such as log files) across all of your different network components and elements. Keep lots of history at the detailed transaction level.
- Integrate social and mobile consumer data to identify and quantify changes in customer, network, and market preferences and behavioral tendencies.
- Augment data assets with external data sources such as weather, local events, holidays, and local economic data to provide new predictive metrics that can improve the predictive capabilities of capacity planning and resource scheduling models.
- Use advanced analytics to project network capacity requirements (at the node, time of day, and day of week levels, and so on) and calculate key network support variables such as personnel, inventory, replacement parts, and maintenance scheduling.
- Leverage real-time analytics to reallocate network capacity (resource scheduling, ramping up or ramping down cloud resources, and others) to support daily, hourly, and location usage pattern changes.

Being a solutions engineer requires not only a strong understanding of the business problems that your organization is trying to address, but also a strong understanding of the capabilities of new big data and advanced analytics innovations. Applying the six-step solution engineering process helps to ensure that you "deploy the right technology capabilities at the right time to solve the right business problem." Without a detailed understanding of the problem you are trying to solve and a solid foundation in the big data analytics capabilities, you will quickly fall back into the old methods of leading with technology "in search of a business problem."

Reading an Annual Report

I'm a big advocate of leveraging an organization's public documents (such as annual reports and quarterly 10-Q financial filings) and announcements (such as press releases and executive presentations) to uncover big data business opportunities. This section of the book will provide some real-world examples of where to look in an annual report to identify potential big data opportunities, and how to do a quick assessment of how big data might be used to power those opportunities.

I'm always surprised by how few people take the time to read their company's annual report, or search out public statements and presentations being made by senior members of the organization's leadership team. In particular, the "President's Letter to the Shareholders" (or the CEO's letter in some cases) is a gold mine. It is within this section of the annual report that the president talks about all the great things they did for the company over the past year. That usually takes up about 75 percent of the letter and, in my humble opinion, can largely be ignored. It's the last 25 percent of the letter that is most informative because it is here that the president talks about the key business initiatives for the next year. Let's review a few annual reports to see what I mean.

Financial Services Firm Example

Following is an excerpt from a letter to the shareholders of a financial services firm:

> **This year we have crossed a major cross-sell threshold. Over banking households in the western U.S. now have an average of 6.14 products with us. For our retail households in the east, it's 5.11 products and growing.** *Across all 39 of our Community Banking states and the District of Columbia, we now average 5.70 products per banking household (5.47 a year ago).* One of every four of our banking households already has eight or more products with us. *Four of every ten have six or more. Even when we get to eight, we're only halfway home. The average banking household has about 16.* **I'm often asked why we set a cross-sell goal of eight. The answer is, it rhymed with "great." Perhaps our new cheer should be: "Let's go again, for ten!"**

This section of the letter highlights a business initiative to improve customer cross-sell effectiveness in order to reach a goal of 10.0 products per banking household, an increase from the current 5.7 products per banking household. While 10.0 may be a BHAG (Big, Hairy, Audacious Goal!), it is clear that some executive in the organization (likely in Marketing) has been chartered with increasing cross-sell effectiveness.

Here are some examples of how big data could help their cross-sell effectiveness business initiative:

- Use detailed customer financial data on the number and types of accounts held by household, combined with key account information (such as length of account ownership, account balance, and account balance trends) and household demographics data, to create more granular household segments.

- Run analytic models to score these new household segments by their likelihood to buy a specific additional financial product. For example, households who hold these products and are in this demographic group have a certain percentage-likelihood of buying this additional product.
- Develop different models for different combinations of products and household demographics.
- Use social media data from sites such as Facebook, Pinterest, Yelp, and Twitter to identify trends in financial products that might be candidates for cross-product promotions. For example, mortgage refinancing is hot, so look to bundle mortgage refinancing with a home equity line of credit. Run these trends against your household/product cross-sell models to identify direct marketing targets.
- Instrument or tag all of the direct marketing and digital marketing campaigns to see what messaging and offers work best for which audience segments.
- Develop an experimentation strategy for identifying what offers to test with what audience segments. Capture the results in real-time and make in-flight campaign adjustments.

Retail Example

This example uses information gained from a retailer's 2011 annual report. There are at least two sections of the annual report where the company could integrate structured data (such as point-of-sale, inventory, returns, and orders transactions) with unstructured data (such as social media, web log, and consumer comments) to drive their key business initiatives. The following highlights the first section of the letter to shareholders:

> *Our strategy is to provide our members with a broad range of high quality merchandise at prices consistently lower than they can obtain elsewhere.* **We seek to limit specific items in each product line to fast-selling models, sizes, and colors.** *Therefore, we carry an average of approximately 3,600 active stock keeping units (SKUs) per warehouse in our core warehouse business, as opposed to 45,000 to 140,000 SKUs or more at discount retailers, supermarkets, and supercenters. Many consumable products are offered for sale in case, carton or multiple-pack quantities only.*

This section highlights an opportunity where big data could help drive store assortment optimization. In particular, big data could help in the following ways:

- Integrate demographics data and product sales data to forecast optimal store assortment (at an individual store level), and update optimal store assortments more frequently (perhaps weekly) based on local events such as Cinco de Mayo or San Francisco Giants home games.

■ Integrate social media insights with consumer comments (such as those gained from call centers, e-mail, and websites) with store and product sales data to calculate and track the net promoter scores and consumer sentiment for particular stores (by product category or season). Then use this information to identify and act on underperforming stores, products, and product categories.

■ Leverage social media data to identify product and market trends (by store and product category) that can impact pricing, in-store merchandising, and store assortment planning.

■ Test different store assortment options in different stores, capture the results, and make recommendations to optimize store assortment at the individual store and department levels.

The second example from this retail company that follows, highlights the business value of increasing private label sales effectiveness (e.g., increase private label sales from 15 percent of products sold to 30 percent over the next several years).

> *We remain focused on selling national brand merchandise while developing our Private Label brand to enhance member loyalty. After 19 years, our Private Label products now represent 15% of the items we carry, but 20% of our sales dollars.* **We believe that we have the capability of building our sales penetration of our Private Label products to 30% over the next several years,** *while continuing to provide our members with quality brand name products that will always be a part of our product selection.*

Here are some examples of how big data could be used to increase private label sales effectiveness:

■ Integrate sales and inventory data with social media data to score product categories that are the most likely opportunities (highest probabilities of success) to introduce private label products. Scores are created by store, geography, and product category.

■ Mine social media data to identify consumers' areas of interest that can be used for direct marketing and in-store promotions and merchandising around promoting private label products.

■ Integrate historic private label sales data and correlate them with local geographic variables including economic conditions, unemployment rate, changes in home sales and home values, traffic conditions, and similar items.

■ Test different private label strategies at different geographic and store levels to determine if certain geographies are more receptive to certain private label product categories.

Brokerage Firm Example

This third example comes from a brokerage firm's 2010 annual report. Following is an excerpt from the letter to shareholders.

> *Client feedback is essential if we hope to see the world through [the] client's eyes. Last year, we continued our Client Promoter Score (CPS) program in which we survey clients and ask them to rate us, from 0 to 10, on their willingness to recommend us. The CPS calculates the number of "promoters" minus the number of "detractors" to arrive at a net indicator of client loyalty.* **Our CPS for individual investors reached a record 37%, with significant gains for our value proposition, investment help and guidance, and customer service.** *CPS scores also remained strong for independent investment advisors, who praised our responsive service, and for retirement plan sponsors.*

The annual report highlights the company's plan to focus on driving their Client Promoter Score (CPS) program. In 2010, the firm was able to achieve their highest score to-date, a record 37 percent. (It would be nice to know if they had a goal and a timeline for their CPS, but maybe that's something that can be determined via interviews.) Here are some examples of how big data can be used to drive the CPS program.

■ Leverage social media sites and blogs to create a more current and comprehensive CPS that is a better predictor of clients' feelings and perspectives (for example, their likeliness to recommend the firm to others).

■ Integrate unstructured customer conversations from call centers, consumer comments, and e-mail received.

■ Build analytic models that incorporate social data and different financial transactions to break out and track CPS by most "valuable" customer segments. Match customer financial transaction patterns with sentiment analysis to flag potential CPS score drops by customer segment.

■ Create analytic models that analyze CPS variables such as broker, brokerage firm, broker location, financial topic, day of week, time of day, and so on. Triage analytic results to uncover any correlations between CPS and broker engagement variables.

- Use the CPS to segment key customers. Leverage Twitter and Facebook data to monitor sentiment trends across their most valuable customer segments in order to more quickly identify and quantify (score) potential customer attrition and corresponding performance drivers.
- Capture key broker demographic (background, education, certifications, years of experience) and performance (client performance, satisfaction scores) data to model the correlation between broker demographics and customer CPS.
- Create real-time tracking control charts that are constantly monitoring key broker engagement variables for potentially troubling situations. Create control charts at the different broker engagement levels, such as broker, broker location, brokerage firm, and financial topic.

You've considered the business transformational power of big data—the power to tease out new customer, product, and market insights that can be used to drive higher-fidelity, more frequent business decisions. But in order to drive business transformation, you need to "begin with an end in mind" (to steal from Stephen Covey). You need to invest the time to understand your organization's key business initiatives, and contemplate the "realm of the possible" with respect to the big data business drivers (for example, more detailed structured data, new unstructured data sources, real-time/low-latency data access, and predictive analytics). There is no better place to start your big data journey than by targeting the key business initiatives that can be found in your company's annual report.

Summary

This chapter introduced you to the concept of solution engineering and provided a six-step process for going from opportunity identification to solution implementation. I provided several examples across different industries, highlighting how a business solution could leverage new sources of data and new big data technology innovations.

You then learned how to read an annual report (and other publicly available data sources) to identify an organization's business initiatives where big data can provide material financial impact. You then reviewed several examples of reviewing annual reports across different industries to identify how big data could impact those organizations' key business initiatives.

11 Big Data Architectural Ramifications

This is the part of the book that most everyone has been waiting for—the technology discussion. As you can probably guess, there is a reason the technology discussion is near the end of the book: a technology discussion can only be productive if it has the benefit of a prior understanding of the business drivers and the targeted business solution around which to scope the technology discussion. Too many times in this industry the first discussion is about the technology features. The reason why organizations want to talk about the technology is because it's easy to talk about its general features and capabilities (the "feeds and speeds") as compared to taking the time to understand what business challenges or opportunities an organization is trying to address with the technology. As is typical in this industry, we're always in search of the "silver bullet."

So this chapter briefly introduces some of the new big data technologies, and provides links and suggested readings in case you want to dive deep into the technologies—there are plenty of outstanding and freely available resources that talk about the new big data technologies. The remainder of the chapter then focuses on exploring the architectural ramifications of big data, especially for organizations that have already made significant investments in their data warehousing and business intelligence (BI) capabilities. As discussed in Stage 1 of the Big Data Business Maturity Index, those business processes around which organizations have already built their data warehouses and BI capabilities are good starting points for the big data journey.

Big Data: Time for a New Data Architecture

For the past 15 to 20 years, organizations have been operating with the data architecture that was built on Online Transaction Process (OLTP)-centric relational database technologies. This architecture worked just fine when dealing with gigabytes and low terabytes of structured data in batch mode, and business users became accustomed to data request turnaround times measured in weeks or months. But there wasn't much "intelligence" in the BI tools with, and very little predictive analytics and data mining capabilities. Reports and dashboards that monitored performance with a rearview mirror view of the business were state of the art (see Figure 11-1).

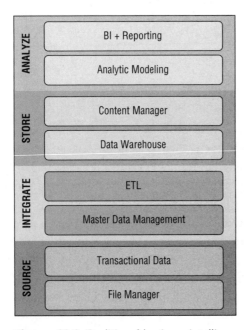

Figure 11-1 Traditional business intelligence/data warehouse reference architecture

- Batch oriented, with high latency
- Monolithic, with inflexible layers
- Brittle and labor intensive (metadata jailhouses)
- Focused on structured data
- Performance and scalability challenged
- Information integration requires significant hand-coding
- Data stored in aggregated tables for specific reports

However, we all know the story by now—Internet companies like Google, Yahoo!, and Facebook couldn't make this architecture work. They explored traditional data management and analysis tools from the traditional data and BI vendors, but even doing things like trying to dynamically tinker with their software kernels to accommodate real-time analysis across hundreds of terabytes and petabytes of data didn't work—and certainly didn't scale. Even if the traditional data vendors could have made this work, the costs associated with their licensing models were debilitating to companies whose business models were driven by the monetization of web visitors and advertising dollars.

As a result, a new generation of data management and analysis capabilities were developed, and many were developed as open source projects so that all developers across these nimble and innovative companies could update and grow the capabilities of this data management and analysis tools faster than any one single vendor. The demands of such next generation companies gave birth to the scale-out data and analytics architecture, and a plethora of new special-purpose software applications (see Figure 11-2).

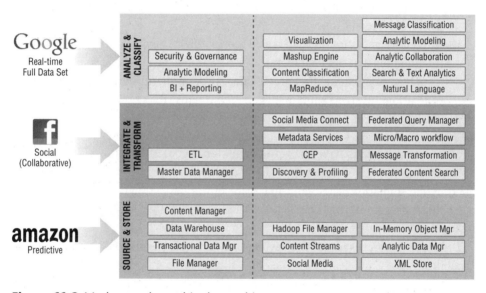

Figure 11-2 Modern, scale-out big data architecture

Introducing Big Data Technologies

These big data technologies have the potential to dramatically re-invigorate your existing data warehouse and BI investments with new capabilities and new architectural approaches. Organizations have an opportunity to extend their existing data warehouse and BI environments by leveraging the following big data capabilities:

- Storage, access, and analysis of massive volumes (meaning hundreds of terabytes and petabytes of data) of structured transactional data (such as sales, orders, shipments, point-of-sale transactions, call detail records, and credit card transactions) at the lowest level of granularity
- Integration of semistructured data (for example, web logs, sensor, GPS, and telemetry data) and unstructured data (such as text fields, consumer comments, documents, and maintenance logs) that can add new dimensions, dimensional attributes, and metrics to your existing data warehouse and BI reports, and dashboards
- Real-time data feeds coupled with real-time analytic environments for capturing, analyzing, flagging, and acting on abnormalities in the data as it flows into your organization
- Predictive analytics that can create scores, forecasts, propensities, and recommendations that can be integrated into your key business operational systems (such as financial, call centers, sales, procurement, marketing, and other operational systems) and management systems (for example, alerts, reports, and dashboards)

Many organizations have the transformational goal of becoming a "real-time, predictive" enterprise. These capabilities, outlined above, are the key enablers for making that transition. They can transform your organization from a retrospective, batch, business monitoring system to a predictive, real-time, business optimization system.

Let's briefly review some of the key big data technologies that are powering these capabilities.

Apache Hadoop

Apache Hadoop is an open-source software framework that supports data-intensive, natively distributed, natively parallel applications. For many, Hadoop has become synonymous with big data. It supports the running of applications on large clusters of commodity hardware using a scale-out architecture. Hadoop implements a computational paradigm named MapReduce where the application is divided into many small fragments of work, each of which may be executed or re-executed on any node in the cluster. In addition, Hadoop provides a distributed filesystem (called the Hadoop Distributed File System, or HDFS) that stores data on the compute nodes, which provides very high-aggregate bandwidth across the cluster. Both MapReduce and HDFS are designed so that node failures are automatically handled by the framework. It enables applications to work with thousands of computation-independent computers and petabytes of data. The entire Apache Hadoop "platform" is now commonly considered to consist of the Hadoop kernel, MapReduce, HDFS, and a number of related projects including Apache Hive, Apache HBase, and others.

> **NOTE** The Apache Software Foundation is a community of developers and users organized for the purpose of coordinating a portfolio of open source projects, and promoting the development and use of open source products, many of which will be described in this chapter. You can learn more about the Apache Software Foundation at `http://www.apache.org/`.

Hadoop MapReduce

MapReduce is a programming model for processing large data sets with a parallel, distributed algorithm on a cluster. A MapReduce program comprises a `Map()` procedure that performs filtering and sorting (such as, sorting students by first name into queues, one queue for each name) and a `Reduce()` procedure that performs a summary operation (such as, counting the number of students in each queue, yielding name frequencies). The *MapReduce System* (also called *infrastructure* or *framework*) orchestrates the distributed servers, running the various tasks in parallel, managing all communications and data transfers between the various parts of the system, providing for redundancies and failures, and managing the overall process. Figure 11-3 shows how the MapReduce function works.

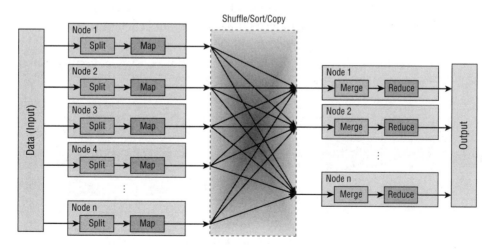

Figure 11-3 MapReduce process flow

Apache Hive

Apache Hive is a data warehouse infrastructure built on top of Hadoop that provides data summarization, query, and analysis. While initially developed by Facebook, Apache Hive is now used and is being enhanced by other companies, such as Netflix. As of the writing of this book, Amazon maintains a software fork of Apache Hive that is included in Amazon Elastic MapReduce on Amazon Web Services. Apache Hive supports analysis of large data sets stored in Hadoop-compatible file systems. It provides an SQL-like language called HiveQL while maintaining full support for MapReduce. To accelerate queries, Hive provides indexes, including bitmap indexes.

Apache HBase

HBase is an open source, non-relational, distributed database model written in Java. It was developed as part of Apache Software Foundation's Apache Hadoop project and runs on top of HDFS. HBase provides a fault-tolerant way of storing large quantities of sparse data. HBase features compression, in-memory operation, and Bloom filters on a per-column basis. Tables in HBase can serve as the input and output for MapReduce jobs run in Hadoop, and may be accessed through the Java API.

Pig

Pig is a high-level, natively parallel data-flow language and execution framework for creating MapReduce programs. Pig abstracts the MapReduce programming language into a higher-level construct, similar to how SQL is a higher-level construct for relational database management systems. Pig can be extended using user-defined functions, which the developer can write in Java, Python, JavaScript, or Ruby and then call directly from the language.

Figure 11-4 shows a typical Hadoop architecture or ecosystem configuration including many of the components discussed above.

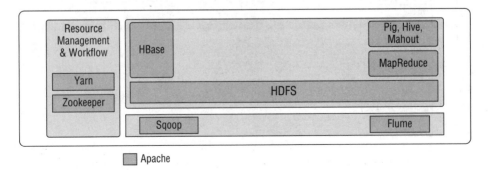

Figure 11-4 Standard Hadoop architecture

NOTE There is a bevy of content on these technologies available on the Apache Hadoop website (http://hadoop.apache.org/). I also recommend reading the book *Hadoop: The Definitive Guide* by Tom White (O'Reilly and Yahoo! Press, 2009). It is the definitive book for those seeking to learn more about Hadoop and the Hadoop ecosystem.

It is worth noting that many vendors are investing heavily to extend the Hadoop functionality to make it easier to leverage Hadoop within an organization's existing data warehouse and BI environments. As of the writing of this book, some vendors such as Pivotal, are adding the capability to access data stored on HDFS directly with industry standard SQL query tools and SQL-trained personnel (see Figure 11-5). I expect this trend to continue.

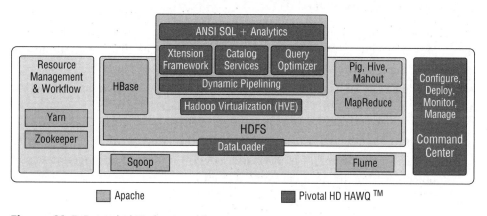

Figure 11-5 Extended Hadoop architecture

New Analytic Tools

There has also been a rash of new development in the area of analytics and data visualization tools fueled by big data. Some of the more interesting tools include:

- R, an open source programming and statistical language that is rapidly gaining popularity among universities and startup companies alike. R is a GNU project, so the software is freely redistributable. Plus it has the advantage of literally thousands of developers using and extending the R capabilities. Go to http://cran.r-project.org/ to learn more about R. And I personally love the RStudio integrated development environment, which opens R to a larger constituency of users. Go to www.rstudio.com/ide/download/ to download and learn more about RStudio.

- Apache Mahout, another Apache Software Foundation project, provides scalable machine learning algorithms on top of the Hadoop platform. Mahout provides algorithms for clustering, classification, and collaborative filtering implemented on top of Apache Hadoop using MapReduce. Go to http://mahout.apache.org/ to learn more about Apache Mahout and see the wide range of analytic algorithms supported by Mahout.

- MADlib, an open-source library that supports in-database analytics. It provides data-parallel implementations of mathematical, statistical, and machine-learning methods that support structured, semistructured, and unstructured data. Go to `http://madlib.net/` to learn more about MADlib.

New Analytic Algorithms

Finally, I don't want to leave out the many innovations that are taking place in the development of new, advanced analytics capabilities. The discussion about the capabilities of these new algorithms is beyond the scope of this book. However, I have provided a partial list below of some of my data scientist friends' favorite new algorithms, along with a link where you can learn more:

- Support Vector Machines are based on the concept of decision planes that define decision boundaries and a decision plane that separates sets of objects having different class-membership (`www.statsoft.com/textbook/support-vector-machines/`).

- Random Forest consists of a collection of simple tree predictors, each capable of producing a response when presented with a set of predictor values (`www.statsoft.com/textbook/random-forest/`).

- Ensemble Methods is a model testing and verification technique that tests multiple models to obtain better predictive performance than could be obtained from any one analytic model (`http://en.wikipedia.org/wiki/Ensemble_learning`).

- Champion/Challenger is another model testing and verification technique where you classify your current analytic model as the "Champion," then challenge the champion with different analytic models where each "Challenger" differs from the Champion in some measurable and defined way (`www.edmblog.com/weblog/2007/04/adaptive_contro_1.html`).

- Confusion Matrix is a specific table layout that allows visualization of the performance of an algorithm (`http://en.wikipedia.org/wiki/Confusion_matrix`).

- Wavelet Transformation is a representation of a square-integrable (real- or complex-valued) function by an orthonormal series generated by a wavelet, commonly used for time-frequency transformations (`https://en.wikipedia.org/wiki/Wavelet_transform`).

- Text mining is a process to mine unstructured information and extract meaningful numerical metrics from the unstructured data, turning unstructured data into structured results (`http://en.wikipedia.org/wiki/Text_mining` or `www.statsoft.com/textbook/text-mining/`).

- Sentiment analysis seeks to determine the attitude of a speaker or a writer with respect to some topic or the overall contextual polarity of a document, such as determining the sentiment towards a movie from a social media feed (`http://en.wikipedia.org/wiki/Sentiment_analysis`).

- Feature Selection is the process of selecting a subset of relevant features for use in model construction especially when the data may contain many redundant or irrelevant variables (`http://en.wikipedia.org/wiki/Feature_selection`).

Finally, the StatSoft Electronic Statistics Textbook website (`www.statsoft.com/textbook/`) is a marvelous source of all things dealing with analytic algorithms.

Bringing Big Data into the Traditional Data Warehouse World

Let's cover a few areas where the big data capabilities and technologies discussed earlier in the chapter have the potential to enhance and expand your current BI and data warehouse environments. These big data capabilities and approaches require you to *think differently* about how you approach your BI and data warehouse environment and architecture. Be open to the possibilities before you!

Data Enrichment: Think ELT, Not ETL

The traditional ETL (extract, transform, load) approach transforms (normalize, align, cleanse, and aggregate) the data from the different source systems prior to loading it into your data warehouse. However, with an ELT (extract, load, transform) approach, you first extract and load the data into a big data environment like Hadoop. Once in Hadoop, you can leverage massively parallel processing to accelerate your existing data transformation processes, and leverage new scale-out data processing capabilities to create new data enrichment algorithms. A scale-out environment lets you *think differently* about how you tackle your data transformation and enrichment processes. Developers need to get past the traditional *scarcity mentality* caused by having limited compute capabilities available as with today's traditional ETL process. Instead, embrace an *abundance mentality* where you can leverage almost limitless processing power to perform your data transformations and create new data enrichment algorithms. Let me give you an example.

In the digital marketing world, organizations employ the ELT process to create new composite metrics that help quantify conversion attribution across different digital media treatments (impressions, clicks, keyword searches, social media posts). These digital marketing organizations are trying to ascertain across which combinations of digital activities—across impressions, clicks, searches, and social media postings—do they attribute credit for a conversion or purchase event? These organizations need to determine which combinations of activities were the most influential in driving the purchase. The results of this analysis are subsequently used by digital marketers to allocate their digital marketing spend and optimize their in-flight marketing campaigns.

This attribution analysis is a very nasty problem, and a perfect candidate for the ELT process because:

- You need to create a "market basket" of all the different digital marketing activities or treatments (such as impressions, clicks, keyword searches, and social media posts) for each individual who made a conversion or purchase.
- Then you could create new frequency (how often?), recency (how recent?), and sequencing (in what order?) metrics across the different marketing treatments for each market basket.
- Next, you analyze each of the market baskets and score the different combinations of frequency, recency, and sequencing to identify the specific combinations of treatments that lead to the conversion or purchase.
- Finally, you want to quantify the results in order to optimize your digital media spend across the different marketing dimensions such as websites, social media sites, keywords, ad networks, audience segments, ad types, dayparts, and similar.

What makes this problem a perfect candidate for the ELT process is that you need to have access to a significant history of raw log files (30, 60, or 90 days of history depending, on the product category). You need to process the entire history of log files to create the composite frequency, recency, and sequencing metrics before you can put them into your analytics environment. This type of pre-processing challenge is difficult with the traditional ETL approach where you might have to parse the entire history for each separate composite metric calculation, but it is a perfect candidate for Hadoop and MapReduce where you can create these new composite metrics in one pass.

Data Federation: Query is the New ETL

Continued advances in the area of data federation and semantic master data management are allowing organizations to extend the data warehouse to access non-data warehouse and external data sources on an as-needed basis. Data federation software tools support the concept of accessing and virtually integrating data from disparate data sources, without having to permanently move the data to a centralized data repository or data warehouse. And a Semantic Master file provides the definitions, taxonomies, and linkages (e.g., access methods and protocols) to enable the seamless and virtual access to these virtualized data sources.

This "virtual data warehouse," can support an organization's need to get quick access to infrequently accessed data sources *without* having to go through the weeks- or months-long process of integrating that data into the enterprise data warehouse. This data can be accessed and analyzed virtually, as if the data is physically stored in a centralized data repository. If it is decided later that this is a data source that needs to be analyzed more frequently, then it is still best to bring frequently accessed and analyzed data sources into the centralized data environment from an analytic performance and data management perspective.

> **BENEFITS OF DATA FEDERATION**
>
> Some of the benefits of data federation include:
>
> - Quickly extend your data warehouse environment to access infrequently accessed data sources
> - Support one-off business analytic requests
> - Test and validate business use cases prior to moving into the enterprise data warehouse

Software vendors are developing technologies that index data sources external to the data warehouse and that facilitate access to that data on an as-needed basis.

This is similar to the way in which Google indexes the entire Internet in order to provide sub-second search results to its hundreds of millions of users. This is a powerful technology enabler because it means that business users don't necessarily have to wait for a data warehouse to be updated to handle special one-off reporting and analysis needs. Figure 11-6 shows an overview of the typical data federation components.

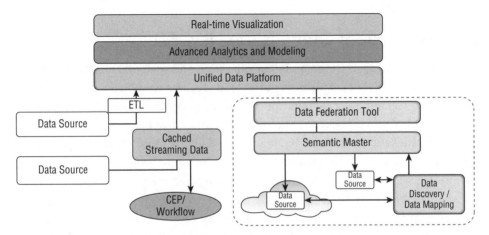

Figure 11-6 Data federation

NOTE   For large scale statistical and machine learning analytic modeling, you need large data sets to feed the model and, as a consequence, data federation is not a good fit. You don't want to move terabytes of data virtually or "on demand."

Data Modeling: Schema on Read

The HDFS supports "schema on read," which means that instead of being forced to define a data schema prior to loading data into your data repository, you instead dump the raw data as-is into your data repository and then define the schema as you query the data.

NOTE   A data warehouse is "schema on write" where the developer must define the data schema prior to loading data into the data warehouse.

The "schema on read" concept has the following benefits:

- Massive data sets can be ingested quickly. You don't have to worry about formatting the data prior to loading it, you just dump it into the data repository as-is. This is especially beneficial when dealing with semistructured and unstructured data sources such as text files, audio, video, and graphics.
- You have much greater flexibility in defining the appropriate schema structure based on the queries you're asking. The problem with today's "schema on write" is that the schema structure may not be optimal for the different groups that are trying to access that data, such as sales, marketing, finance, R&D, or engineering. To accommodate all of these different user types, you end up with a "Franken-Schema" that delivers a bit of something to everyone, but likely not the right schema for anyone.
- If the ingested metadata changes (for example, a new data element suddenly shows up in the source system) the process doesn't stop and you don't lose anything. The new data element would just be consumed and analyzed later on.

This "schema on read" technique is possible because of new data management technologies such as Hadoop and NoSQL. There is a bit of performance degradation in the query process, but given the ability to unleash a massive number of commodity nodes against any particular query request (either via a massively parallel processing architecture or a cloud implementation), you can overwhelm the performance degradation problem with raw, scale-out computing power.

The biggest challenge to "schema on read" is that the query language is much more complicated because the developer will need to include logical and existential conditions for the metadata in addition to the descriptive logic for the data. To make things worse, each technology has its own language. There is no standard yet.

Hadoop: Next Gen Data Staging and Prep Area

One of the early Hadoop use cases for extending an organization's existing data warehouse and BI environment is a next generation data staging and data preparation area. This architectural addition brings the following benefits:

- The ability to ingest and store massive amounts of data as-is, at a cost that is typically about 95 percent less than the cost of a traditional data warehouse. Regardless of the structure of your incoming data (structured, semistructured, unstructured, audio, or video), you can rapidly load and store all the data in Hadoop as-is, where it then becomes available for your ETL, data warehouse, BI, and advanced analytic processes.

■ You can leverage the natively parallel capabilities of Hadoop to perform traditional ETL data transformation and alignment work more quickly and cheaply. This can significantly accelerate your traditional ETL processes and the service level agreements (SLAs) you have with your business users. Plus, you shrink the latency between when the data transaction or event occurs and when it's available to your ETL, data warehouse, BI, and advanced analytics processes.

■ You can embrace new data enrichment techniques that were not possible with traditional ETL processes. For example, you can parse unstructured data sets (such as consumer comments, web logs, or social media feeds) to create new metrics, dimensions, and dimensional attributes that can be fed into your enterprise data warehouse.

■ Hadoop provides the foundation for self-provisioning of an analytics sandbox environment. Within the analytics sandbox, the data scientists can grab whatever data they need out of the Hadoop data staging area without worrying about impacting the data warehouse production environment and related SLAs. The data scientists can select whatever level of granularity they need in the data, from whichever data sources they need, in order to build, test, and refine their analytic models.

Figure 11-7 summarizes these benefits.

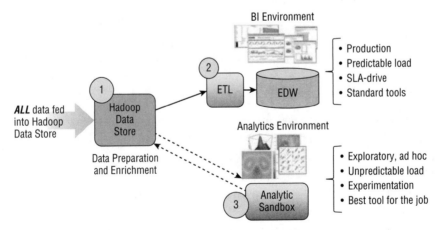

Figure 11-7 Hadoop next generation data staging

As you can see, using Hadoop as your next generation data staging and preparation area can deliver new, compelling business benefits—not to mention that it's probably significantly cheaper and more agile then your existing ETL environment. You're going to start seeing more use cases for Hadoop within your ETL, data warehouse, BI, and advanced analytics environments. The cost benefits, processing power, access to lower-latency data, and overall simpler architecture are just too compelling to ignore.

MPP Architectures: Accelerate Your Data Warehouse

Massively Parallel Processing (MPP) databases provide a cost effective, scale-out data warehouse environment that allows organizations to leverage Moore's Law on performance-to-cost improvements in x86 processors. MPP databases provide a scale-out data warehouse and analytics platform for data discovery and exploration on massive amounts of data. Built on inexpensive commodity clusters, MPP databases can extend, complement, and even replace parts of your existing data warehouse, managing massive volumes of detailed data while providing agile query, reporting, dashboards, and analytics (see Figure 11-8).

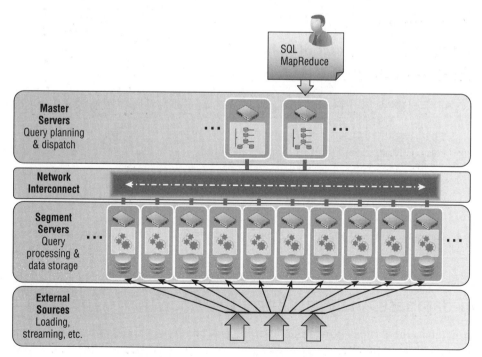

Figure 11-8 Massively Parallel Processing (MPP) databases

NOTE Moore's Law, which is named after Intel co-founder Gordon Moore, states that computing power doubles about every 18 months at the same price point thereby producing a fairly predictable and compelling economic benefit. The economic power of Moore's Law can be appreciated if one applies Moore's Law to other industries, such as if airlines had followed Moore's law from 1978, that airline tickets would cost $0.01 and the flight would take one second.

Characteristics of an MPP architecture include:

- MPP architectures provide massively scalable, shared-nothing, scale-out data platforms running on commodity processors
- Provides automatic parallelization
- All nodes can scan and process in parallel
- Linear scalability by just adding more nodes

An MPP data warehouse will enable access to more granular data for query, reporting, and dashboard drill-down and drill-across exploration. Analysis can be performed on detailed data instead of data aggregates. Recent developments now allow you to build your data warehouse directly on the HDFS to benefit from the cost efficiencies, scale-out architecture, and native parallelism provided by HDFS, while providing access to the HDFS-based data warehouse using the organization's standard SQL-based BI tools and SQL-trained business analysts.

BENEFITS OF MPP ARCHITECTURES

One of the benefits of MPP architectures is being able to leverage more detailed and robust dimensional data. Examples include:

- Seasonality to forecast retail sales and energy consumption
- Localization to pinpoint lending or fraud exposure and support location-based services
- Hyper-dimensionality for digital media attribution or healthcare treatment analysis

In-database Analytics: Bring the Analytics to the Data

In-database analytics addresses one of biggest challenges in advanced analytics: the requirement to move large amounts of data between the data warehouse and analytics environments. That has caused many organizations and data scientists to have to settle with working with aggregated or sampled data because the data transfer issue is so debilitating to the analytic exploration and discovery process. In-database analytics reverses the process by moving the analytic algorithms to the data, thereby accelerating the development, fine-tuning, and deployment of analytic models. Elimination of data movement with in-database analytics results in substantial benefits:

- Under today's conventional (without in-database analytics) approach, the entire analytic model development and testing can take hours. For example, if a data scientist needs to move 1 TB of data from a five-processor database server to the analytical server at 1-gigabyte per second and then run the analytic models, the entire process would take 193 minutes for just one iteration of the model development and testing.

- However with in-database analytics (where the data scientist can run the analytic algorithms directly in the database without having to move the data to a separate analytic environment), the entire analytic development and testing process can be reduced dramatically. Because moving data is the most time-consuming activity, reducing data movement (courtesy of in-database analytics) reduces the processing time by 1/N, where N is the number of processing units. Consequently, the analytic model development and processing time for 1 TB of data can be reduced by a factor of 16 (using the same five-processor system), going from 193 minutes to 12 minutes. This means that the data scientist can more quickly iterate on the model testing, theoretically creating a more accurate, more thoroughly vetted analytic model as a result (see Figure 11-9).

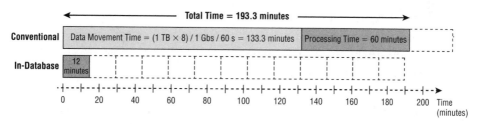

Figure 11-9 In-database analytics

On the analytics side, once a model has been developed and business insights have been gleaned from the data sets, having the data warehouse environment and the analytics environment on the same MPP platform will simplify migrating the analytic model and analytic insights into the data warehouse and BI environment.

BENEFITS OF IN-DATABASE ANALYTICS

One of the benefits of in-database analytics is being able to leverage low-latency (real-time) data access to create more timely analytic models. Examples include:

- Drive real-time customer acquisition, predictive maintenance, or network optimization decisions
- Update analytic models on-demand, based on current market or local weather conditions

Cloud Computing: Providing Big Data Computational Power

Cloud computing, with its shared compute and storage resources, software, and data, provides the ideal big data platform. A big data-ready cloud platform supports (a) massive data management scalability (from terabytes to petabytes of data), (b) low-latency data access, and (c) integrated analytics to accelerate the advanced analytics modeling. Cloud technologies allow you to build a platform-as-a-service environment that enables application developers to rapidly provision development environments and dramatically speed the operationalization of the analytic results. And all of these capabilities are available on-demand, supporting both the reoccurring and the one-off computing and analysis requirements of the business.

A big data ready cloud-computing platform provides the following key capabilities:

- **Agile Computing Platform**: Agility is enabled through highly flexible and reconfigurable data and analytic resources and architectures. Analytic resources can be quickly reconfigured and redeployed to meet the ever-changing demands of the business, enabling new levels of analytics flexibility and agility.
- **Linear Scalability**: Access to massive amounts of computing power means that business problems can be attacked in a completely different manner. For example, the traditional ETL process can be transformed into a data enrichment process creating new composite metrics, such as frequency (how often?), recency (how recent?), sequencing (in what order?), n-tiling and behavioral segmentation.
- **On-Demand, Analysis-Intense Workloads**: Previously, organizations had to be content with performing cursory "after the fact" analysis; they lacked the computational power to dive deep into the analysis as events were occurring or to contemplate all the different variables that might be driving the

business. With a cloud platform, these computationally intensive, short-burst analytic needs can be exploited. Business users can analyze massive amounts of data, in real-time, to uncover the relevant and actionable nuances buried across hundreds of dimensions and business metrics.

Summary

This chapter began with a discussion of the transition from a traditional ETL, data warehouse, and BI environment to a modern, big data-ready data management and analytics environment.

Next, you were introduced to some of the key big data technologies (Hadoop, MapReduce, Hive, HBase, and Pig) and considered some of the new data management and analytics capabilities being enabled by these new technologies. The chapter wrapped up with a discussion of how some of these new big data technologies, capabilities, and approaches can be used today to extend and enhance an organization's existing investment in ETL, data warehousing, BI, and advanced analytics.

12 Launching Your Big Data Journey

Data has always been the fuel that powers insightful business thinking. Leading organizations have historically leveraged data and analytics to identify and act on market opportunities faster than their competitors. But in the world of big data and advanced analytics, data has assumed a front-and-center role in transforming key business processes and creating new monetization opportunities. Big data, with access to rich sources of web, social media, mobile, sensor, and telemetry data, is yielding new insights about customers, products, operations, and markets. Leading organizations are using these insights to rewire their value creation processes, provide competitive differentiation, and drive a more relevant and profitable customer experience.

This book provides tips, techniques, and a "how to" guide—complete with worksheets, sample exercises, and real-world examples—to help organizations:

- Identify where and how to start their organization's big data journey.
- Uncover opportunities to leverage big data capabilities and technologies to optimize existing business processes and create new monetization opportunities.
- Drive collaboration between the business and IT stakeholders around a business-enabling big data strategy.

This chapter uses the Big Data Storymap (Figure 12-1), which has been provided courtesy of EMC, to summarize the key observations and strategies presented in this book.

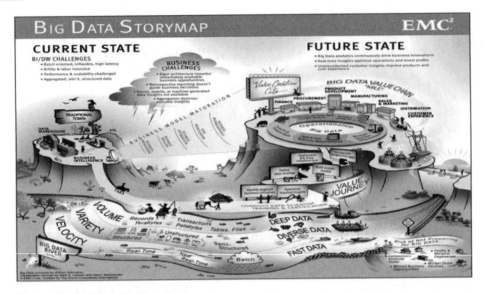

Figure 12-1: Big Data Storymap

The goal of the Big Data Storymap is to provide a graphical visualization that uses metaphors to reinforce some of the key big data best practices necessary to create a successful big data strategy. The ability to articulate an engaging story is critical to winning the confidence of your business and IT stakeholders in order to get them on-board for the big data journey. Through the use of visualizations filled with themes and metaphors, you can tell that story. And like any good map, there are important "landmarks" that you want to make sure you visit.

Explosive Data Growth Drives Business Opportunities

Data powers the big data movement. Big data is deep and insightful, wide and diverse, and fast and powerful, and can lead to new business insights from the ability to:

- Mine social, mobile, and other external data sources to uncover customers' interests, passions, associations, and affiliations.
- Analyze machine, sensor, and telemetry data to support predictive maintenance, improve product performance, and optimize network operations.
- Leverage behavioral insights to create a more compelling user experience.

Organizations are learning to appreciate data, and are expanding processes to capture, manage, and augment their data. As a result, they are learning to treat data as an asset instead of a cost. Organizations are also starting to grasp the competitive advantage provided by their analytic models and insights, and are starting to manage those analytics as intellectual property that needs to be captured, refined, reused, and in some cases legally protected. Organizations are learning to embrace and cultivate a data or analytics-driven culture—letting the data and analytics guide the decision-making instead of tradition and the most senior person's opinion (Figure 12-2).

Figure 12-2: Explosive data growth drives business opportunities.

Market dynamics are also changing due to big data. Massive volumes of structured and unstructured data, a wide variety of internal and external data, and high-velocity data can either power organizational change and business innovation, or it can swamp the unprepared. Organizations that don't adapt to big data risk:

- Profit and margin declines
- Market share losses
- Competitors innovating faster
- Missed business opportunities

Traditional Technologies and Approaches Are Insufficient

Big data is about business transformation. Big data enables organizations to transform from a "rearview mirror" hindsight view of the business using a subset of the data in batch to monitor business performance, into a predictive enterprise that leverages all available data in real-time to optimize business performance. Unfortunately, traditional data management and analytic technologies and approaches are hindering this business transformation because they are incapable of managing the tsunami of social, mobile, sensor, and telemetry data, and consequently, they are unable to tease out the business insights buried in those data sources in a timely manner. As depicted in Figure 12-3, traditional data warehouse and business intelligence (BI) technologies impede business growth because:

- They cannot store, manage, and mine the massive volumes of data—measured in petabytes—that are available from both internal and external data sources.
- They are unable to integrate unstructured data—such as consumer comments, maintenance notes, social media, mobile, sensor, and machine-generated data—into existing data warehouse infrastructures.
- They use data management techniques built on data aggregation and data sampling that obfuscates those valuable nuances and insights buried in the data.
- They are unable to provide real-time, predictive analytic capabilities that can uncover and publish actionable business insights in a timely manner.
- Their batch-centric process architectures struggle to uncover those immediately available, on-demand business opportunities.
- Their retrospective reporting doesn't provide the insights or recommendations necessary to optimize key business processes.

Figure 12-3: Traditional technologies and approaches are insufficient.

The Big Data Business Model Maturity Index

What are your organization's aspirations with respect to leveraging big data analytics to power the value creation process? What business processes are best suited to exploit these big data capabilities? How do you leverage your customer, product, and operational insights to create new monetization opportunities?

Chapter 1 introduced the Big Data Business Maturity Index which can be used to benchmark an organization's big data business aspirations (Figure 12-4). The index provides a pragmatic "how to" guide for moving your organization through the following stages of business maturity:

- **Business Monitoring**: Deploy data warehousing and BI to monitor the ongoing performance of your current business processes.
- **Business Insights**: Integrate unstructured data, real-time data feeds, and predictive analytics to uncover actionable insights and generate recommendations that can be integrated into key business processes.
- **Business Optimization**: Leverage advanced analytics, operational instrumentation, and experimentation to create optimization models that can be integrated into existing business processes.
- **Data Monetization**: Leverage customer, product, and operational insights to create new revenue opportunities by repackaging and reselling key business insights, creating intelligent products by integrating insights into physical products, or leveraging customer and product insights to create a more compelling and profitable customer user experience.
- **Business Metamorphosis**: Leverage customers' usage patterns, product performance behaviors, and market trends to transform an organization's product-centric business model into an ecosystem strategy that empowers others to make money from your analytics-enabled platform.

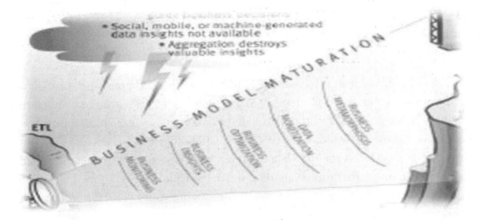

Figure 12-4: Big Data Business Model Maturity Index

Driving Business and IT Stakeholder Collaboration

To be successful, the big data journey requires collaboration between the business and IT stakeholders to identify where and how to start the big data journey (Figure 12-5). This book provides a methodology and several examples for using the Vision Workshop process and the Prioritization Matrix methodology for driving business and IT stakeholder collaboration. The methodology enforces a process that moves from solution ideation, to proof of value validation, to production that covers the following steps:

- **Identify targeted business initiative.** Identifies the "right" use cases that have both relevant business value and a high feasibility of implementation success—the "low-hanging fruit" business opportunities.
- **Determine required insights.** Ideally suited for the Vision Workshop process, this step envisions, brainstorms, and prioritizes the business insights necessary to support the targeted business initiative.
- **Define data strategy.** Identifies the supporting data strategy including data sources (internal and external; structured and unstructured), access methods, data availability frequency and timeliness, metrics, dimensionality, and instrumentation.
- **Build analytic models.** Identifies, builds, and refines the supporting analytic models embracing many of the analytic tools and algorithms introduced in

Chapter 11. Also useful to develop an ongoing experimentation strategy and process.

- **Implement big data architecture.** Builds out the necessary architecture addressing ETL/ELT, data staging area, data management platform, master data management capabilities, business intelligence and advanced analytics platforms.
- **Incorporate insights into apps.** Addresses the application development requirements and architecture to ensure that the analytic models and insights can be operationalized into the production systems and management applications.

Throughout the big data journey, the organization will want to conduct data scientist training and certification (as an example, see `https://education.emc.com/guest/campaign/data_science.aspx` for more details about EMC's data scientist training and certification).

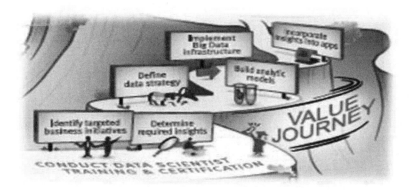

Figure 12-5: Driving business and IT stakeholder collaboration

The big data journey accelerates big data adoption by creating the business case, proving out the analytic models, and building the financial justification around your targeted business opportunity.

Operationalizing Big Data Insights

Successful organizations define a process to continuously uncover and publish new insights about the business (Figure 12-6). To be successful, organizations need a well-defined process to tease out analytic insights and integrate them back into their operational systems and management applications. The process needs to clearly define the roles, responsibilities, and expectations of key stakeholders, including business users, the data warehouse team, the BI team, the user experience team, and data scientists. This book outlines an operational process that:

- Drives collaboration with business stakeholders to capture ongoing business requirements.
- Acquires new structured and unstructured sources of data from internal and external sources, and then prepares, enriches, and integrates the new data with existing internal data sources.
- Continuously refines analytic models and insights, and embraces an experimentation mentality to ensure ongoing model relevance.
- Publishes analytic insights back into operational systems and management applications.
- Measures decision effectiveness in order to fine-tune analytic models, business processes, and applications.

Figure 12-6: Operationalize big data insights.

Big Data Powers the Value Creation Process

Big data holds the potential to transform your organization's value creation processes. Organizations need a big data strategy that links their big data aspirations to their overarching business strategy and key business initiatives (Figure 12-7). Throughout this book, examples have been provided of how an organization can leverage big data and advanced analytics to enhance the value creation process in business areas such as:

- **Finance**: Identify which line-of-business operations and product categories are most effective and efficient in driving profitability.
- **Procurement**: Identify which suppliers are most cost-effective in delivering high-quality products on time.
- **Product Development**: Identify product usage insights to speed product development and improve new product launches.
- **Manufacturing**: Flag machinery and process variances that might be indicators of quality problems.
- **Marketing**: Identify which marketing campaigns are the most effective in driving leads and sales.
- **Distribution**: Quantify optimal inventory levels and supply chain activities.
- **Customer Experience**: Deliver a more relevant, more personalized customer engagement that drives long-term customer loyalty, advocacy, and profitability.
- **Operations**: Optimize prices for "perishable" goods such as groceries, airline seats, and fashion merchandise.
- **Human Resources**: Identify the characteristics of the most effective employees.

Figure 12-7: Big data powers the value creation process.

Summary

The Big Data Storymap provides a comprehensive and engaging metaphor around which to end this book (go here: www.wiley.com/go/bigdataforbusiness if you would like to download a PDF version of the Big Data Storymap). It helps to nurture that natural curiosity about what big data can mean to your organization, and helps you to envision the realm of what's possible through a visual story. It summarizes many of the key big data best practices in a single graphic (see Figure 12-1) that you can share with your key stakeholders as you build the organizational support for your big data journey. You are now ready to launch your own big data journey. Go forth and be fruitful!

13 Call to Action

Now that you've studied all the materials, techniques, methods, and worksheets in the book, let's summarize all of the action items from the different chapters into a single call-to-action checklist. This checklist will help prepare your organization for the big data journey by addressing the specific actions that you can take to leverage big data to power your organization's key business initiatives, optimize your key business processes and uncover new monetization opportunities. This checklist puts you on the path to understanding how data powers big business.

Identify Your Organization's Key Business Initiatives

- Identify, research, and understand your organization's key business initiatives and key business opportunities.
- Leverage publicly available sources to triage your organization's key business initiatives. Sources include annual reports, quarterly analyst calls, industry research and publications, executive presentations, and competitive activities.
- Leverage the Big Data Strategy Document to break down your organization's business strategy into its key business initiatives and the supporting key performance indicators (KPI), critical success factors (CSF), desired outcomes, execution timeframe, key tasks, and business stakeholders.
- Begin with an end in mind.

Start with Business and IT Stakeholder Collaboration

- Big data is about business transformation. Consequently, there must be a close collaboration between business and IT stakeholders from the very beginning, even starting with joint big data education activities.
- Ensure that your big data initiative is relevant, meaningful, and actionable to the business stakeholders, and that they understand what the big data initiative will do for them from a business enablement perspective.
- Leverage Vision Workshops and envisioning exercises to build partnerships between the business and IT stakeholders.
- Make sure the workshops and the supporting envisioning exercises are tailored to the organization's specific business initiatives and opportunities.
- Formalize a process for business stakeholder on-going involvement, feedback, and big data initiative direction.
- Establish an on-going working relationship built around constant collaboration between business stakeholders and IT and use of Vision Workshops to ensure that the big data journey delivers compelling and differentiated competitive advantages.
- Welcome new ideas.

Formalize Your Envisioning Process

- Establish a formal envisioning methodology, like the Vision Workshop, that helps the business stakeholders envision the realm of what's possible with big data.
- Develop facilitation skills.
- Leverage organizational data—both internal and external to the organization—to build business-specific envisioning exercises.
- Brainstorm how the four big data business drivers could empower the business questions that the business users are trying to answer and the business decisions that the users are trying to make.
- Leverage Michael Porter's Value Chain Analysis and Five Forces Analysis to tease out big data ideas and use cases.
- Leverage the Prioritization Matrix to gain group consensus on the next steps while capturing the key business drivers and potential project impediments.

- Use analytic labs as a tool for building the business case and proving the value of the analytics.
- Challenge conventional thinking.

Leverage Mockups to Fuel the Creative Process

- Create user and customer experience mockups to make the analytic insights gleaned from big data *come to life* for the business stakeholders.
- Exploit mobile app and website mockups, as they are an especially effective communication and engagement vehicle with your customers, consumers, and partners.
- Leverage mockups to envision how you can present new customer, product, and operational insights in a manner that drives a more compelling and profitable customer experience.
- Don't underestimate the power of a superior user experience to drive new monetization opportunities.
- Use PowerPoint as an easy-to-use and quick mockup tool; don't waste time trying to make mockups perfect.
- Have fun.

Understand Your Technology and Architectural Options

- Don't let existing data warehouse and business intelligence processes, which are insufficient for today's deep, wide, and diverse data sources, hold you back.
- Leverage new technologies, such as Hadoop, in-memory computing, and in-database analytics, to provide new data management and advanced analytics capabilities, and open up new, more modern architectural options.
- Be prepared to embrace open source technologies and tools within your environment; open source is the new black.
- Create an architecture that separates the service level agreement (SLA)-driven, production-oriented data warehouse/business intelligence environment from the exploratory, ad hoc, rapidly evolving data science environment.

- Data will have more lasting value than the applications that generate that data. Don't let your existing applications hold your data captive.
- Don't wait for your traditional technology vendors to solve your business problems for you—take the initiative and start the journey now.
- Don't throw away your data warehouse and business intelligence investments—build off of them.
- Become a real-time, predictive organization.

Build off Your Existing Internal Business Processes

- Leverage your existing data warehouse and business intelligence investments that support your key business processes. This business intelligence effort has already captured the data sources, metrics, dimensions, reports, and dashboards surrounding key business processes.
- Move from business monitoring to business optimization.
- Look for opportunities to expand on existing business processes by leveraging the organizational *dark* data (that is, your existing transactional data that is not being used to its fullest potential), new internal and external unstructured data, real-time data feeds, and predictive analytics.
- Integrate predictive analytics into your existing business processes to automatically uncover actionable insights buried in the wealth of detailed, structured and unstructured data. The traditional business intelligence approach of "slicing and dicing" to uncover actionable insights doesn't work against terabytes or petabytes of data.
- Make instrumentation (that is, tagging each of your customer engagement points to capture more data about your customers and their behaviors) and experimentation part of your data strategy.
- Look for opportunities to leverage big data to rewire your value creation processes.

Uncover New Monetization Opportunities

- Leverage the customer, product, and operational insights that result from upgrading your existing business processes to create new monetization opportunities.

- Understand that monetizing your customer, product, and operational insights can take numerous forms, including packaging the insights for reselling, integrating the insights to create "intelligence products," and leveraging the insights to create a more compelling, engaging and profitable customer experience.
- Look at what other industries are doing and how they are leveraging big data to make money.
- Move beyond the "3 Vs of Big Data" (volume, variety, and velocity) to embrace the "4 Ms of Big Data"—Make me more money!

Understand the Organizational Ramifications

- Create an analytic process that seeks to uncover and publish new business insights by integrating the data scientist role with that of the business user, data warehouse, and business intelligence teams.
- Treat data as a corporate asset to be acquired, transformed, and enriched. Treat analytics as differentiated corporate intellectual property, to be inventoried, maintained, and legally protected.
- Create an organizational mindset that embraces the power of experimentation and fuels the naturally curious "what if" questioning.
- Think differently.

Index